Cookies and Cancer— What a Party!

Cookies & Cancer— What a Party! The Story of Victory in the Valley, Inc.

Copyright © 2025 Diana K. Thomi and Janet M. Eldridge

ISBN 13: 979-8-218-68268-2
Library of Congress Control Number: 2025909540

Edited by Laura Hambrick and Elizabeth Boerner
Layout and Cover Design by Helen Ounjian
Photography credit: Chris Engle-Tjaden, Certified Forensic Photographer who
donated his time and expertise to provide photographs for the book
Front cover image by Mariusz Blach for Adobe Stock

**Our deepest thanks to Sheryl Freeman, our friend and author who
tremendously helped us by reading and editing the early manuscripts. Her
expertise in writing and organizing was invaluable. Thank you, also to Sue
Wineinger who read early drafts and made helpful suggestions.**

Perfect Misfits LLC
An Independent Publishing Company
For inquiries, contact perfectmisfits.de@gmail.com

Perfect Misfits LLC
An Independent Publishing Company

# Cookies
## and Cancer-
## What a Party!

The Story of
Victory in the Valley, Inc.

Diana K. Thomi
with Janet M. Eldridge

Lois Joy Thomi, founder of Victory in the Valley (Diana's Mother)

Dear Mommy Thomi (as others often called her),

Growing up, I often found myself wanting to be like you! I would observe the way you interacted with people, whether in business or friendship, and it was clear that you treated everyone equally. You genuinely cared about everyone, brought laughter and smiles to their faces, and offered encouragement, helping them through their challenges while facing your own.

You truly embraced life, even during the toughest times. You were the most incredible teacher I could have asked for when it came to understanding life and how to live it fully. You approached challenges with such strength and grace, often discovering joy in the little things that many overlook. You always kept a healthy perspective, choosing not to focus on the difficulties but instead seeking to rise above them. Even when you didn't have much, you never felt jealous of others; instead, you were grateful and content for what you did have. You had an amazing ability to find humor, even when you were hurting, and your laughter was infectious, bringing joy even to those who may have caused you pain.

You kept your eyes on God, trusting Him to guide you through the tough moments in life. Instead of dwelling on your own challenges, you chose to reach out to others with genuine care and concern for their well-being.

If you were here to read this, you might feel inclined to say that you were not "that good," but everyone who truly knew you would wholeheartedly agree that you were so much more. I know you were not perfect, but you always managed to carry an attitude of gratitude during life's toughest storms.

Mom, I love and miss you, but I take comfort in knowing we will see each other again. THANK YOU for the incredible legacy you have left for me and so many others!

It is with joy and thanksgiving that we dedicate this book to you, my beloved mother, Lois Joy Thomi.

The Lord is my strength  and my shield;
My heart trusts in Him, and I am helped;
Therefore, my heart triumphs,
and with my song I shall thank Him.

Psalm 28:7 NASB

# 1

"Yes, I'm a nurse... No, I don't want to look at it." This humorous quote is on a favorite mug in my kitchen. It captures the reality of the many times nurses are approached by apprehensive and worried friends, as well as strangers, with questions and concerns about a spot, lump, or rash.

Single and living in west Wichita, I was never far from dropping by the Union Rescue Mission, where my parents worked, to see how they were doing. I graduated from the Wesley School of Nursing in 1970 and worked there as an RN. Life went on for many years, with Mom and Dad settling into their routines at the Mission while I grew comfortable in my routine as a nurse.

In May 1982, my fellow nurse and friend, Charlene Jantz, and I were working together at Wesley Medical Center. By that time, I had become a head nurse. We had the opportunity to attend a medical conference in Chicago, and we were excited to gain new information that we could apply to our department. My cousin

Patricia, whom we called "Pat," lived in the Chicago area with her husband, and when she learned we would be in her area, she encouraged my fifty-five-year-old mom to join us and invited her to stay at their home. Mom was particularly close to this niece and was thrilled to catch up on their lives and enjoy their generous hospitality. Pat's husband was a vice president of Motorola, and their elaborate home featured an indoor swimming pool, which was perfect for Mom, for she loved to swim.

Mom rarely traveled alone, and even when it was their vacation, she and Dad did not fly. (Dad claimed he had had enough of flying during WWII.) However, this time, Mom convinced Dad that it was a great opportunity for her to reconnect with her family and escape the stresses of work. He agreed to let her go on the trip, even though they had planned a two-week vacation for early June, which was just a month away.

How exciting! Mom, Charlene, and I were together on the plane to Chicago, enjoying a few days visiting Pat. Charlene and I stayed at the hotel and conference center while Mom enjoyed shopping and dining out with Pat, who treated her like royalty. After our conference ended, we spent a day with Mom and my cousin. When it was time to leave, Pat hired a limousine service to take us to the airport. We were not used to such luxuries (especially when it wasn't for a funeral!). We enjoyed the ride, waving to kids who seemed to think we were very important, possibly a movie star or someone very wealthy. If only they knew!

The reality was that Mom and Dad's lives revolved around living and working at the Rescue Mission, leaving little time for leisure. None of us had experienced such luxuries as fine dining, shopping, and accommodations that we were now enjoying at my cousin's generous expense.

We returned home from Chicago early in the day, and after we landed, we went our separate ways. I went home to unpack and told Mom I would be back later to fill Dad in on the details of our trip. After unpacking and taking care of a few things at my house, I returned to the mission apartment where they lived and sat with my folks to enjoy sharing the fun stories from our trip. After lunch, Dad went downstairs to work for a bit while Mom and I stayed in their living room, having "girl talk" and laughing about the funny things that happened during the trip. Mom and I created so many wonderful memories.

All of a sudden, Mom turned a bit serious, yet not overly concerned, and said, "Honey, I want to ask you something." She continued, "I want to show you this spot." She began to undo her blouse and added, "I found this red spot on my breast and wondered if you thought it was from overdoing it at the swimming pool?"

My mouth went dry. As I looked at it, my nursing instincts kicked in, and I calmly asked, "When did you notice it? Is it painful? Is it warm to the touch? Is it tender?" As the knot in my stomach began to tighten, I told her she probably needed to make an appointment with the doctor soon. It could be many things, such as an infection, but the doctor would need to examine it. She replied that they were looking forward to their vacation in June, so she would make an appointment with her doctor when she returned. Trying not to alarm her while expressing concern, I said, "No... Don't wait until then; do it before you go, so you'll know if it's anything serious, and maybe you can enjoy your vacation without worrying."

Immediately, my thoughts turned to the two young mothers I had cared for in the cancer unit where I had worked. Each experienced the same symptoms as Mom, and as their disease progressed, they were told they had inflammatory breast cancer and that there was no effective treatment for this type of cancer. I played a part in caring for them and watched their decline with great sadness while we did everything possible to keep them comfortable. I tried to convince myself that Mom had always been a picture of health and stamina, pushing away the looming doubts and fears.

Mom took me up on my firm advice, got up from the couch, and right away called her doctor, and was able to schedule an appointment. Their two-week vacation was just over a week away (I was doing my best to hide my panic).

Her appointment was scheduled for the next week, but in the meantime, she was treated with antibiotics in case it was an infection. Mom informed Dad about it that same day, but as usual, she took things in stride and didn't seem to worry, even though she was concerned. We did a lot of praying, especially me, since I thought I knew what the outcome would be. Mom continued working at the Mission, but she noticed that the area on her breast was growing larger rather than smaller. Trying to maintain a "normal" routine was impossible for me. Dad excelled at being the worrier in the family, and we all continued praying. Inside, I was a wreck! As the days passed, I wanted to prepare Mom, but didn't want to scare her until we knew more.

The doctor ordered a mammogram and told her he would call her with the results.

A few days later, I was with Mom when the doctor called. He inquired about the reddened area and informed her that he was referring her to a surgeon for a biopsy. Mom's face turned pale, and she exclaimed, "He is sending me to a surgeon. He thinks it might be serious!" My worst fears were coming true.

I became her "internet" (since there wasn't a "Doctor Google" at that time), so I answered questions carefully. We talked openly about the possibilities, although I still didn't share with Mom what I knew about the probable cancer; instead, I discussed it in more detail with my fellow nurse friend, Charlene. The doctor arranged for Mom to see a surgeon I personally knew. Very slowly, the short time of waiting dragged by.

Arrangements were made at a minor surgery center, and the day of the biopsy arrived. Dad and our best friends, Jack and Dorothy Tomman, accompanied us to the surgery center. Dorothy stayed with me in the waiting room while the biopsy took place. Dad, who never did well in medical situations, and Jack took a short walk around the block to talk and pray during the biopsy. The surgeon we had chosen was excellent and highly respected. I knew him well and was grateful that he would be caring for Mom.

Jack and Dorothy Tomman - (best friends of Glenn & Lois)

After what felt like days, the doctor came out of surgery and asked to speak with Dad and me in private (never a good sign).

He led us to a private room, and I was fairly certain I knew what was coming. He said, "She has a rare and very aggressive type of cancer. It's Inflammatory Breast Cancer."

Then he looked at me and said, "You know what that means, don't you, Diana?"

He finished by saying, "I stayed over to see her as a favor to you, but I have a plane to catch, so someone will need to tell her what we found."

I felt paralyzed, but I knew that, as a nurse, this responsibility had fallen to me. My thoughts were jumbled as I processed the facts while trying to manage my emotions. It's one thing to believe you understand what it is and another to hear it aloud, as if that somehow makes it more real.

Jack and Dorothy had been our best friends since I was five. I considered them my second mom and dad, and since they had no children, they also viewed me as part of their family. It was comforting to have them with us during this trying time.

After the nurse came out of the recovery room, she said we could go back and see Mom. Jack and Dad stayed in the waiting room, trying to digest the news. Dorothy,

Mom's best friend since childhood, and I went back into the recovery room. Mom was wide awake and glad to see us. She looked at me and asked, "Did you get a report?" I nodded, trying to find my voice. "Yes, Mom, we did." She looked at me with fear in her eyes and asked, "Is it bad?"

All I could do was nod.

She asked, "Real bad?" I found my voice and said, "Yes, Mom, you have cancer." She closed her eyes, and a single tear rolled down her cheek.

I felt a wave of emotions that I cannot adequately express. I felt scared, sad, angry, and terrified, as though I had just given my mother her death sentence: my own mother, my *best friend*.

## The diagnosis of cancer began the journey of a lifetime.

I helped her get dressed, and we left without much conversation. What was there to say? Was this the moment to share sentimental thoughts or make encouraging statements like, "You will be fine," or other empty words that seem to lack substance?

As is often the case, our journey with cancer began unexpectedly, without any preparation or warning. The security of a routine life pattern was lost in the panic of uncertainty. At the time of the diagnosis, we were engulfed by a maze of instructions with no sense of direction or guidance. Suddenly, our schedules changed moment by moment as a mountain of tests was scheduled or rescheduled for different dates and locations. X-rays, scans, labs, meetings with her oncologist, consultations with the surgeon, visits to the radiation doctor- the list went on and on. Everything was arranged for her, and it felt like life was out of our control... and *it was!*

At the same time, we wondered why no one seemed to be in a hurry to get Mom into appointments immediately-like yesterday! Why were they scheduled so far in advance? Didn't they know that *we* have CANCER? We didn't understand at the time that the treatment centers were trying to be accommodating. Treatments are scheduled based on the availability of the doctor or the treatment center's timetable. Don't they know that WE have special occasions on *our* calendars for *them* to work around?

Instead of going on a planned vacation, Mom was undergoing tests and learning about the "enemy within."

## Suddenly, our world had been turned upside down, and nothing would ever be the same again!

I am sure this nightmare happens to many patients. You lose your ability to make plans to attend events or activities, as you don't know what tests or treatments may be scheduled for you. If you have started chemotherapy, you aren't sure how you will feel from day to day. Treatment often alters your taste, so when people ask what food they can bring, you can't decide because you don't know what will taste good at that moment. Everyone knows about you, but some people avoid you because they are unsure of what to say. The uncertainties of treatment are frightening, especially at first.

## Isn't it true that we often feel the need to run faster when everything seems out of control?

Then, there is the anger at the unfairness of cancer. My mom had already experienced severe trauma, growing up with an abusive, alcoholic father. Instead of following in his footsteps, she spent her adult life helping and serving others. Why was this happening, of all people, *to her?*

A page from Lois Joy's journal:

> *"Being raised in a home where my father was controlled by alcohol was not easy. I was the middle one of nine children. My days were filled with anxiety because when my dad was drinking, he often brutally mistreated our mother. I remember sitting in my grade school classroom with my eyes on the pages of my book, pretending to be studying, but instead, wondering if my mother was all right at home. Since I was the oldest child living at home, as soon as school was out, I would hurry home to make sure my mother and younger brothers and sisters were all right. Instead, I*

Lois Thomi (her mother & siblings)

would often find my dad in a drunken stupor, perhaps after locking my mother outside, throwing dishes or other breakable household items at her, or beating one of the other kids.

We lived in a house my dad had built but never quite finished. Partitions were up, but we could walk through them to all of the other rooms. We kids slept in an unfinished basement, and the girls' bed was right under our parents' bedroom. Often, Dad would come home drunk and would cause all kinds of ruckus before he would go to bed. When he finally wore down, he would sit on the edge of his bed and take off his shoes. When we heard his shoe drop, we knew he was going to stop for the night, and everything would be okay for a while.

Years later, my parents divorced, and all of my brothers and sisters had grown up and worked in various professions….one was a chemist, another was a CPA, two were ministers, two were attorneys, and I began work in retail management. I had married and had a daughter, and I thought the days of my fear, anxiety, and dread were behind me. But little did I know that one day, the 'shoe would again drop,' and this time, it didn't seem like anything would ever be okay again!"

One day, after her diagnosis, I sat in the kitchen at the mission while Mom rushed to prepare a meal for the men staying there. She was weary but still faithful. I looked out the window and saw a couple of guys who were drunk and fighting each other while Mom, tired yet persevering, worked hard to prepare a meal for them! It wasn't fair that *she* had cancer, and it made me angry. Why her? Why did one of the happiest, kindest, funniest women I knew have to get cancer? And where is God in all this? Why did He allow it?

## We often feel so alone while surrounded by people.

Since I had worked with the medical oncologist (cancer doctor) that Mom was to see, I asked him many questions. What drugs would he give her? How effective were they for her type of cancer? What was his anti-nausea regimen? Most importantly, what was the success rate for Inflammatory Breast Cancer? His answers hit me hard, even though I was fairly certain about what he might say. "There isn't one," he said quietly but factually. I then asked if we should take her to MD Anderson Cancer Center or the Mayo Clinic, and he replied, "If someday you and your dad look back and wish you had tried, then go ahead, but the treatment will probably be the same." There it was... *NO* HOPE!

Glenn & Lois Thomi (Diana's parents)

# 2

My parents, Glenn and Lois Thomi, met at a skating rink in McPherson, Kansas, in 1947. Dad had just returned home after completing his service in World War II. Mom often joked that Dad "fell for her" because he wasn't a good skater. They married in McPherson and moved next door to Dad's parents' home, into a small house converted from a garage. Mom initially worked as a telephone operator. Some of you may remember picking up a telephone and hearing, "Number, please." For those who don't know, operators were used because there were no dials or buttons on phones.

Later, Mom managed Montgomery Ward stores. Dad became a plumber, and I came onto the scene in 1948.

Since I was an only child, there were no siblings to help or hinder me. When I was little, my mom would buy me dolls made of hard plastic—you know the kind. On the other hand, my father would buy me toy cap guns. In order to please both of them, I would line my dolls up and shoot them!

Every evening, when Dad got home from work, he played with me until Mom had dinner ready. Dad would get down on his knees, and we would pretend we were boxing. I would "hit" him, and he would fall over backward as if I knocked him out! We would laugh and laugh; then he would end up tickling me, and we would do it all again. Afterward, he would raise my hand as if I were the champ! (I'm sure he was hoping that dinner was almost ready!)

Sometimes, I would place my feet on top of his boots, and we would take giant steps around the house! Because he was a plumber, his boots always had a bad smell, so Mom was not happy that my bare feet were exposed to his dirty boots. But we had fun. Later, as I grew older, I would help him work on the car. I felt so important!

My mother's middle name was Joy, and it suited her perfectly. She was a happy and fun-loving person whom everyone adored. Mom had a wonderful sense of humor and was always the center of attention, not because she sought it but because others hung on her every word and laughed along with her wherever she was. Mom inherited her wonderful sense of humor from her mother.

My grandmother instilled in my mother and her siblings the importance of focusing on the positive aspects of life while encouraging them to laugh at themselves along the way. She taught them to cultivate gratitude, which ultimately contributed to their success despite the challenges of growing up with my grandfather, a severely alcoholic father.

My dad had a completely different personality from my mom. As the youngest of seven siblings, he often felt the need to be in charge, perhaps because his brothers and sisters always told him what to do. When he couldn't control a situation, it frustrated him since he couldn't "fix" it, and he occasionally became angry over minor issues; he was never mean but would become excessively irritable about things we thought were insignificant.

He was born on a farm in Burns, Kansas. At the age of eight, he contracted tuberculosis, and since there was no treatment available except in a specialty hospital, hours away from home, he was admitted for several months. No family members were allowed to accompany him, so he was there without anyone he knew. It was a very traumatic time for him. I believe that, in some ways, his experiences as a young child shaped how he dealt with Mom's cancer during her illness. He was there for her, but did not want to stay in the facilities any longer than necessary.

One Sunday, at the age of 18, he was in a movie theater in McPherson when WWII broke out, and as a young man, he was soon drafted into the Army. For 18 months, he found himself in the thick of battle in Europe as a spotter, identifying enemy airplanes for the gunners to shoot down. When he was discharged, he returned home to McPherson, KS. It was no wonder that he often wrestled with fear and worry.

My dad and mom were friends with many other couples, so Saturday nights became a regular get-together with friends to have drinks and socialize. We never went to church, much to my grandparents' dismay. On some Saturday nights, when everyone gathered, I would go to each person and ask if I could have a taste of their drink (I was only 5). If Mom saw me making the rounds, I would be sent to bed right away. (Boy, I really slept well on those nights!)

Dad began to think about their life priorities, worrying that their lifestyle was influencing me too much (he often remarked later that he questioned whether I would end up drinking excessively like he did). He believed they needed to attend church for my benefit. One Sunday, we visited a church that was forming, and Dad realized that his life needed to change. That day at church, he became a Christian and gave his life to Christ.

Actually, both my parents became Christians in 1953, and our lives began to change. Dad was never one to put on airs and consistently lived his life with no apologies. Instead of hosting parties on weekends, he became a fully committed and devoted follower of Christ—sometimes perhaps a bit extreme, but always faithful. He wanted to serve God in every way possible, which later led to a lifetime opportunity in rescue mission work.

He was ordained as a minister in 1955 and mainly worked and served as the Director of Rescue Missions in several states. He could understand and relate to the men who diluted their lives in alcohol, as well as many who lost their jobs, families, and even professional careers.

One example I vividly remember is of a doctor in another state who was very successful. He came home one day to find that his entire family had been murdered. He began to drink heavily and, in a short time, lost everything- his home, his practice, and he started to wander from state to state and mission to mission. Even though Dad had not experienced such profound devastation, he understood and cared. Mission work suited his personality and the experiences from his past.

Over the years, my parents served in numerous missions in Texas, New Mexico, and Wichita. While Mom worked in retail management at Montgomery Ward, she managed stores across the United States as we moved. She was so successful that the company offered her a position at the corporate office. After many years of mission work, our family returned home to McPherson and pursued jobs outside of mission work. By this time, I was in high school. In 1966, during my senior year, Dad received a call to apply for the Director of the Union Rescue Mission position in Wichita. He applied and was hired, which meant another move for us. However, he was excited to return to the work he loved. Mom and Dad allowed me to stay behind in McPherson and live with friends until I graduated from high school, after which I moved to Wichita.

People would often ask where my parents lived in Wichita. Mom would smile and say, "We have a high-rise apartment in downtown Wichita." Nothing could be farther from the truth! She would then clarify that they lived in a small apartment on the second floor of the Rescue Mission. Each evening, after a day of secretarial work, followed by cooking and serving dinner to the men staying there, she would slowly climb the long stairs to their apartment on the second floor. They loved serving at the Rescue Mission; however, it was also difficult because they could never escape from work. They served approximately 2,000 people each month.

Across from their apartment, on the same floor, was the dormitory where the men stayed. Many of the men were homeless individuals who came inside for the night to take a shower and sleep in a bed. Others were professionals, such as doctors and lawyers, who, due to some horrible tragedy in their lives, turned to alcohol and lost everything, often including their families. Still others were felons and escapees.

We once had a man stay at the mission for a few nights before he traveled to Chicago. My parents later saw his picture on the news: he had *murdered* seven student nurses in Chicago *after* staying with us! He had been sleeping only a few yards from where my folks slept, with just a couple of doors between them. Can you imagine??

My folks' "high-rise apartment" was simple yet clean, with a small kitchen, a small bathroom with a very old tub and a bedroom with a bed that squeaked whenever you turned. This was their home for twenty years, as Mom and Dad served the men who were the guests of the Mission.

Mom was fun, but she could be quite firm when necessary. She loved everyone, regardless of their background. One day, a woman living in a low-income apartment nearby came into the small discount store run by the Mission. She had a simple job and bought clothes at the Rescue Mission store. Someone had made and donated a quilt for the store to sell and keep the profits. The quilt was pretty enough, but it was crafted for warmth rather than decoration. This lady often came to buy a blouse for a dime or other small items, and each time she visited, she would admire the quilt.

This continued for almost a year, and the quilt just didn't sell. Mom felt sorry for her, knowing she was a hard worker doing her best to care for herself and not rely on anyone else. One day, the lady came in again, admiring the quilt. Mom quietly went over, took it down, folded it up, and gave it to her. The lady couldn't believe it and was overwhelmed with appreciation for Mom, who had shared God's love with her. She was almost floating out the door, holding the quilt lovingly in her arms. Sadly, several months later, her apartment building caught fire, and the lady was trapped and tragically died in the flames. Mom used that as an example: when God impresses you to do something, *do it*!

When Mom served food to the men at the mission, she sometimes teased them, and they teased her back. She treated them like friends. There were scary moments though, as occasionally, a drunk man would pull a knife or hold a gun to her head and threaten to kill her. No one else was often around, but God gave her wisdom and protected her. My favorite response she used when threatened was, "You put that away now! What would your mother say if she saw you acting that way?" Often, at the mention of their mother, the guy would drop the weapon and begin to cry and apologize! Mom would smile and take it all in stride. It was her wonderful sense of humor and caring heart that carried her through the tough times.

By the time Mom turned fifty, she suffered from arthritis in her joints. However, at the mention of going shopping or out to lunch, she transformed into a "quick change artist" and was ready to go.

In the late 1960s, while attending the Wesley School of Nursing in Wichita and living in a dormitory, I would visit the Mission on Saturdays, spend some time with my dad, and then Mom and I would hit the stores. Since the Mission was located in downtown Wichita, we would walk to the nearby shops. Our favorite was Macy's, where we would browse the latest styles and maybe try on shoes, but our "shopping" rarely involved buying anything.

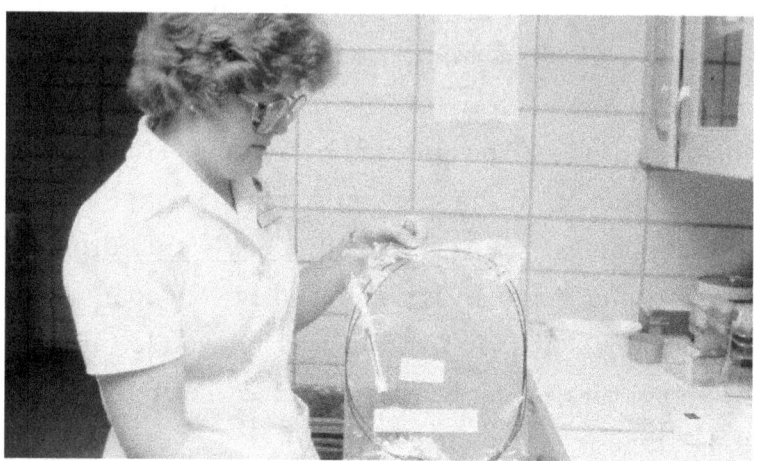

Diana Thomi – nursing career

Mom was often asked to present at women's events and large gatherings because she was an excellent speaker. She cared about looking her best. You could always tell when she had a speaking engagement because she would wear her nicest clothes and add a spritz of Estée Lauder Youth Dew (her one splurge). She called it her "French Perfume that rocked the room," and she was right about that—except it wasn't French!

Mom was my best friend, so while we were "hitting the stores," we would talk. We shared our frustrations and hurts, but always our joys as well. We laughed until we could hardly take another step, regrouped, and then shopped some more. I must say those moments were the most important and precious times for us. We usually ended up having a light lunch and then walking back to the mission so she could prepare the evening meal. She insisted that the men be served good meals, even if it consisted of just beans and side dishes. The food she cooked for them was what we all ate, and she served it with joy and even a bit of fun.

We couldn't go shopping during the holidays because there was so much to do. Mom would start preparing a full traditional Thanksgiving meal a few days prior. On Thanksgiving day, she would wake up around three a.m., go downstairs to the mission kitchen, where she would put about three turkeys in the oven, peel pounds of potatoes, and prepare some type of vegetable, salad, and dessert. She wanted those who stayed at the mission to enjoy a traditional holiday meal. Sometimes, friends or people from church would come and help finish preparing and serving the meal.

Dad would preach before the Thanksgiving meal. Sometimes, I would pause my kitchen duties to play the piano for the service and then return to the kitchen. After the service concluded (and Mom made sure Dad wouldn't go over time), we would serve the usual sixty-plus people their Thanksgiving meal. Sometimes, there would be as many as 100 people! After our Mission guests finished eating, we would clean up, and anyone helping us would sit down and eat together. Often, we would share the things we were thankful for before eating, but sometimes, we were just so tired and hungry that we hoped the person saying grace would keep it brief! After serving and smelling the delicious food, we were ready to eat, which made us truly grateful.

Mom cherished her quiet time and her coffee. Each morning, she would read her Bible. She woke up early to make a pot of coffee. Once it was ready, she poured herself a cup and settled at the cozy kitchen table. From there, she gazed out the window at the city stirring to life and offered a silent prayer. After her first cup of coffee, she poured another and began reading her Bible along with her daily devotional. She reviewed the previous day's devotional page, noting something she wanted to remember or a blessing. Then, she wrote a note for the upcoming day.

Mom had a favorite devotional book that she read faithfully alongside her Bible. I never really understood why she loved that particular devotional, but she always seemed to draw encouragement from it. Much later, I read what remained of the tattered book and was amazed at the significance of its pages. The book *Streams in the Desert* was written by Mrs. Lettie Cowman, a pioneering missionary in Japan and China. First published in 1925, it remains in print today.

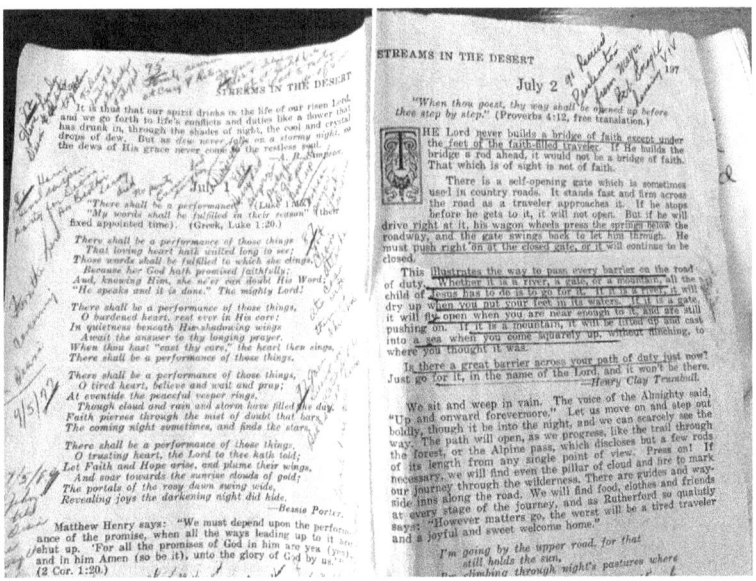

Devotion book of Lois (Streams in the Desert) – Illustrates how she wrote her notes/prayers

Mrs. Cowman compiled her devotional book during her husband's terminal illness, and the outcome has brought comfort to countless readers facing difficult times. For Mom, living and working at the Rescue Mission was not an easy job, but it provided a prophetic glimpse into her days ahead. The words of the devotional book became encouragement from one woman's heart to another.

Based on Isaiah 43:19, *Streams in the Desert* represents a part of God's promise to His people:

"Behold, I am about to do something new: even now it is coming…indeed, I will make a way in the wilderness and streams in the desert." This Scripture reminds us that when we face difficult days, God goes before us, making a way through our struggles while caring for us and our needs. This was certainly true in our lives, as Mom had no idea what lay ahead.

After finishing her reading, Mom would start getting ready for her day. She would dress, do her hair and makeup, and then go downstairs to begin her workday. No two days were the same; however, she would always wear a lovely dress, as she knew she would be greeting visitors, some who wanted information and others who were perhaps dropping by to donate something. She would then start cooking in preparation for the evening meal, which she would serve to the men. Once that began, she would go to her office and tackle the tasks that needed to be completed, whether writing letters, making calls, or handling other paperwork.

Dad would be up a little later. He would dress and go down to the Mission's kitchen, where he usually had toast and coffee. He would then check to see if something urgent needed attention before going to his office to make calls, plan sermons, or attend to whatever the day held for him.

There was a routine, and no two days were the same; they were normal to us. Life was how it was.

However, we could not prepare for what was ahead.

God had other plans.

# 3

Our cancer journey began not with preparation and confidence but with uncertain baby steps surrounded by fear. Mom was admitted to the hospital for testing before starting treatment on the very day they were supposed to leave for vacation. Her oncologist met with us and explained that she would receive a combination of two chemotherapy drugs, and the treatments would last for at least a year, depending on her response to the medications. Next, we were referred to a radiation oncologist at Wesley Medical Center for an evaluation. Due to the aggressiveness of her tumor, her oncologist outlined a treatment plan consisting of two months of chemotherapy, followed by six weeks of daily radiation treatments, a mastectomy, and then another year of chemotherapy. The implication was that "if" she lived that long. This treatment plan was unusual for that time, but God had a hand in all of the decisions.

Thankfully, Mom had insurance, so after a brief discussion, we were relieved knowing that her care and treatments would be fully covered.

(PLEASE NOTE: With advances in treatment and the development of new, more effective drugs, treating Inflammatory Breast Cancer is different today. Mom was treated with the best options available in the early 1980s.)

A day later, Mom was admitted to the oncology floor of the hospital. Testing would begin and continue until it was completed and reviewed by the oncologist. After an intense day of tests, Mom was resting in her hospital room when she heard about a meeting to answer questions about cancer. She decided that she needed as much information as possible, so she planned to attend. This educational session was to be held down the hall from her room. Although she felt tired, she slowly walked down the hallway to the meeting. Everything about her experience so far was overwhelming, and she didn't know what to expect or what questions to ask.

The room where the meeting was held was filled with cancer patients and their caregivers, each eager to learn how to confront the enemy they were battling. The meeting started, and they were informed that the topic of discussion was "How to Plan Your Funeral." Slowly, the crowd began to dwindle as fear and disappointment took hold of their hearts and minds. No one was interested in learning how to plan a funeral when they were all fighting so hard to learn *how to live!*

It is interesting how a crisis can change your life. Often, we get caught up in the "everyday" aspects of living—where to go, what to do, and what someone said to you, whether good or bad, and the list goes on. When a time of crisis comes, everything can change quickly to focus on what REALLY matters, while the trivial things that once seemed so important become mere "fluff" that hardly matters at all. For example, one of Mom's friends who traveled to Europe brought her back a collectible Hummel porcelain figurine. She had received several of these earthly treasures and always enjoyed looking at them tucked safely away in her cabinet. Suddenly, after her diagnosis, the Hummels became significantly less important to her. Although she remained grateful for them, she became much more appreciative of the friends who had given them to her.

When I returned to the hospital, Mom told me about the meeting and how she had left early with many of the other attendees. Mom was angry about the topic they announced but also empathetic toward the other cancer patients present. They expressed regret that the subject of the meeting had depressed them instead of helping them.

I wanted to do something to encourage Mom. I asked if she was hungry and what I could bring her. She told me the only thing that sounded good was pizza from Angelo's (one of our favorite restaurants) and Rocky Road ice cream. Wanting to do something special for her, I quickly went to get the pizza and ice cream and brought them to her in the hospital. We tried to have a happy feast, hoping that something would feel normal again. After we had eaten our fill- and much to our dismay- the nurse came to our room to tell Mom she was starting her first chemo in just a few minutes. Let's just say Mom never really enjoyed pizza and ice cream for a very long time after that.

The treatment began shortly afterward, and one of the biggest challenges at that time was the limited availability of anti-nausea medications. There were only two basic anti-nausea drugs available, one of which is still occasionally used in combination with newer, more effective medications. For Mom, one of the two available drugs had the opposite effect, making her nervous and shaky without alleviating her nausea at all. After each treatment, she would vomit, and when there was nothing left in her stomach, she would dry heave for hours, unable to tolerate even a sip of water. I felt so helpless that nothing worked to manage her nausea, yet it is wonderful that the newer anti-nausea drugs are so effective today. Unfortunately, those drugs were not yet available for Mom.

As a nurse, I stayed with my mom in the hospital. She depended on me for information and assistance. She appreciated this support because I was able to explain what was happening, which brought her great comfort and allowed her to relax while experiencing the effects of chemotherapy.

Dad also relied on me to help Mom during this time. Due to their differing personalities, he handled this stressful situation in his own way. Mom was accepting, while Dad struggled more with anxiety and fear of the future without her. He also hated to see Mom struggle, so he stayed home while she was in the hospital and prayed. I was relieved, as he likely would have been feeling unwell too! He didn't cope well in hospital settings, and I didn't want to care for *two* patients.

Mom battled the side effects of chemotherapy month after month, and each treatment ended the same way. If you are currently undergoing chemotherapy, I want to reassure you that today's anti-nausea medications are remarkable and highly effective. Very rarely does anyone become ill during treatment. Most people now receive treatment as outpatients, managing the side effects more easily. Some patients are able to go out to eat after treatment. Although others may not feel their best, at least they can attempt to eat and drink despite the challenges posed by a poor appetite and taste changes that often accompany chemotherapy. The key is to take the anti-nausea pills as soon as your stomach starts to feel "off," rather than waiting to see if you will get sick. It is much easier to prevent nausea than to try to catch up after realizing that you are feeling really sick.

During the times when Mom was in the hospital for treatment, she began meeting other cancer patients and their families, who would ask her questions about her experience while sharing their journeys as well. They started seeking her out for information and encouragement, asking if it would be possible to gather and help one another find answers. Mom, who had a compassionate heart, told me she had been visiting patients in the treatment room while receiving her own treatment. She mentioned that many of them had questions about cancer and its side effects. One lady was crying and said she was "losing her hair and wondered if it would ever grow back." Another person wondered if it was possible to "catch cancer from someone." Other patients encouraged others to go to Mexico to obtain Laetrile for cancer treatment! One individual passed around a book that claimed you should eat nothing but almonds when you have cancer. (Mom informed them that her doctor had told her she might have a short time to live and that she couldn't eat that many almonds!) One man mentioned that he had undergone chemotherapy for his treatment and that his doctor wanted him to proceed with radiation next, which he was reluctant to do. Mom advised him that if he had made it through chemotherapy, radiation would be much easier. He was surprised and said he might need to reconsider.

There was considerable confusion about the various treatments, their side effects, the different types of cancers, and their respective treatments. Cancer patients were looking for the 'one' treatment that could cure all cancers, but it was nowhere to be found. There were desperate individuals filled with many questions, yet few answers. As Mom shared her knowledge, people found some help and encouragement, realizing that others had the same or similar questions and understanding that they were not alone.

Many patients and their families wanted to know if it was possible to meet so they could learn how to cope with all of the life changes and to support one another. After several treatments and opportunities to connect with other cancer patients, Mom realized she was also benefiting by sharing her experiences with them. At that time, it was a completely different world of uncertainties, and aside from the doctors and other medical professionals, they found encouragement through their shared experiences. The idea of hosting people in her home to discuss questions about cancer was the farthest thing from her mind, as she was sick, anxious, and praying just to LIVE!

The doctors I worked with when we received her diagnosis did not say much to me, as I think they did not want to upset me. Her prognosis was grave. They confided in my friend Charlene and asked her not to tell me, but they essentially said that Mom was going to die.

Another nurse friend of mine was aware of Mom's diagnosis, and I shared with her what was happening, looking to her for hope and encouragement. She asked if I thought my dad would remarry and remain in the ministry after Mom passed away! I was appalled. It upset me that she would ask such a question when we were all working so hard to help her live. Much later, when I told Mom what my friend had said, she replied, "That's why I got well!"

Soon after Mom's diagnosis, I decided to move back home to help care for her due to her poor prognosis. Dad appreciated the company but soon felt the urge to control an uncontrollable situation. He cared deeply for Mom but struggled to express and cope with his feelings. Confronted with the possibility of losing her, he felt increasingly helpless, fearful, and out of control.

Mom preferred to drive herself to radiation treatments, but Dad would take her when she didn't feel well. He struggled emotionally with her condition and often felt unwell in certain medical environments. Therefore, Mom appreciated being able to visit the doctor independently to ask her questions and receive answers. She managed the harsh realities of her cancer without falling apart. This arrangement seemed beneficial for both, as Dad would stay home, pray for her, and tackle chores like vacuuming and doing the dishes until he received a call to pick her up.

The hardest thing to watch was that Mom could not get any relief from the nausea and vomiting, so she really could not eat, even though it wasn't for lack of trying. After a few days, the nausea would subside, and we would try to help her catch up on her eating, as long as we didn't mention pizza or a certain flavor of ice cream.

During this time, she was receiving her chemo treatments at her oncologist's clinic instead of the hospital. Mom was growing very weary, and it was rare for her to feel discouraged, but she was quiet, and that was unlike her.

The phone rang; it was Kansas Attorney General Bob Stephan. He was a friend of my mom's brother, as well as a cancer survivor. My uncle informed him about Mom's cancer diagnosis. She later revealed that she was at her lowest point of her journey that day since receiving the diagnosis. Attorney General Stephan advised her that if she listened to her doctors, followed her treatment, and prayed, God would help her through it. The right words spoken at the right time made all the difference!

I could never have imagined what the future would hold. My only thoughts were to do everything I could for my mom and to pray that, by some miracle, she might live.

# 4

I loved being a nurse and working at Wesley Medical Center, where I had trained. Although I held positions in several areas, my favorite was working with cancer patients. With the development of new chemotherapy and nausea medications, cancer care became an evolving science, with ongoing improvements in treatments that resulted in less severe side effects. I was thrilled to see that they were conquering the side effects and developing treatments that were extremely effective therapies.

In my earliest days in oncology, I remember the physicians treating cancer patients with very few drugs and limited care available at that time. Communication with patients and family members regarding cancer and specific treatments was basic and extremely limited.

During that time, we nurses accompanied the doctors on rounds as they visited their hospitalized patients. Visiting those with cancer was especially challenging. If a patient's blood counts dropped so low that they were at high risk for infection, our only recourse was administering antibiotics and placing them in "reverse isolation," a series of precautionary measures designed to protect the patient from contracting illnesses from staff and visitors. This meant the patient was placed in a private room, and all visitors were screened for illness. No flowers or live plants could be brought into the room, and all equipment had to be repeatedly cleaned and sanitized. (Standard isolation, on the other hand, aims to protect others from contracting whatever illness the patient may have.) We used to joke that the food served to patients in reverse isolation seemed as if it had been prepared in a sterilizer! It was challenging for them to eat anything, given the nausea and unappetizing food.

There were many questions and few answers, mainly due to numerous unknowns. Most doctors were kind and empathetic, though some were more matter-of-fact. It was difficult for them to connect emotionally while delivering challenging news. The nursing staff faced similar struggles; we cared but had no answers. We tried our best to support and listen. Often, we served as the gateway to convey information to the family, who sometimes felt left in the dark. Hugs and a listening ear can communicate when words fail.

The hospital administration at Wesley noticed an increase in cancer patient admissions. Since no other medical facility specifically addressed this issue, they established a cancer unit. The general medical floor they selected was the one where I worked as the Assistant Head Nurse. Aware of the dramatic increase in cancer treatment options and eager to provide this specialty, they recruited an oncologist from a cancer hospital in Missouri to help us develop a specialized cancer unit. This physician began teaching us about cancer care, the new chemotherapy drugs that were becoming available, and the medications to manage the side effects. Equally important as the treatments, he educated us on the emotional aspects of cancer.

At that time, Elisabeth Kübler-Ross, a renowned psychiatrist, identified the stages of grief and loss that individuals go through during challenging or crisis situations. Certainly, having a cancer diagnosis is a crisis. According to Kübler-Ross, there are five fundamental stages of grief.

They are:

**Denial:** Experiencing disbelief and panic

**Anger:** Assigning blame to oneself or others

**Bargaining:** Feeling guilt over regrets

**Depression:** Experiencing hopelessness

**Acceptance:** Acknowledging loss and moving forward

As nurses, we began to understand the various emotional stages involved in working with cancer patients. Our goal was to comprehend their fears and expectations, address their questions, and provide encouragement and realistic hope, even if just for that moment. Kübler-Ross, alongside her colleague David Kessler in "On Grief and Grieving" (2005), stated that she never intended for this to be seen as a rigid set of stages experienced by everyone in sequence but rather as a tool to identify some feelings associated with grief and loss. It was certainly not meant for others to evaluate and judge but rather to promote understanding with kindness and compassion.

The need for increased information and support for cancer patients was considerable due to the insufficient communication from medical staff to patients. We all strived to understand how to be more supportive and manage new situations and side effects.

# 5

My parents continued to work at the Mission even after Mom began her cancer treatment. However, Dad soon realized it would be best to retire and leave the Mission. He wanted to buy a house so that Mom could rest instead of having to work. When one of the volunteers at the Mission listed her house for sale, they purchased it, allowing them to move into their own home.

⸙

As Mom continued her monthly treatments at the center, she met more and more cancer patients and their caregivers. Once again, the plea echoed: "We need to come together and support one another through this. There is so much we don't know!" Witnessing and feeling the struggles they all faced, Mom advised them not to expect anything but promised to take their contact information and see if she could find someone to help.

She wrote down their details; over time, the list of patient names grew quite lengthy.

———

As Mom approached the end of a year of chemotherapy treatments, she was making progress, which was somewhat unexpected. Could it be that she was going to live?

———

Always concerned about others, Mom came to me and said, "Look at all these names of people who are going through cancer. They need help! We need to do something for them."

She asked if I would help her put together an invitation and send it to everyone on the list. Then she said, "I doubt anyone will come, but we need to have some refreshments available in case anyone does."

We sent out invitations to come to our home at a specific time to share our questions and concerns about cancer. Refreshments would be provided. (Looking back, we laughed at how silly it seemed to invite others to talk about cancer and eat cookies—*what a party!*)

Thomi house where first meeting was held in 1983

However, Mom's purpose in having this one-time meeting was to ensure that discussions about cancer with other patients and caregivers, cancer and its treatment, would become a little less frightening and overwhelming.

> You start to realize that you are not alone in this journey and discover that together, we'll multiply each other's joys and divide each other's sorrows.

When the appointed day and time arrived, we prepared a plate of assorted cookies and thought that if anyone showed up, we could figure out what to do as we went along. The doorbell rang, and gradually, patients and caregivers began to arrive. Soon, we ran out of chairs. We looked around and realized the room was full! Mom and I were in the kitchen, trying to think of how to handle all the unexpected company. Pretending we had a plan all along (which we didn't), we announced that we wanted to start by giving everyone the opportunity to share their cancer situation or at least just their name.

Mom turned to her right and asked the older gentleman sitting beside her if he would begin by telling her his name. He slowly replied, "I don't have cancer, but my wife, who is sitting across the room, does." He continued, "I'm mad about it! In fact, I'm mad at God!!! So, what do you think of that?" His wife began to cry and said, "I've had cancer for two years, and this is the first time he's ever talked about it." (The room fell silent, and secretly, I thought, "What a way to start the meeting!") Mom took a breath, patted his arm, and said, "God loves you and cares about what you are going through. He promises to go through it with you if you let Him. And we will be with you and your wife too." His wife was so surprised by his words that she began to cry even harder. The lady next to her gave her a big hug. The man started to weep as well and said, "I know it. Thank you!" Mom reached out and patted his arm. I was so grateful that Mom shared those words because I couldn't think of anything to say!

As the sharing continued, the next person was a young man who had recently been diagnosed with a brain tumor.

He had been the principal of a Christian school and had to quit his job because of the tumor. His wife's parents lived in Wichita; her mother was my mom's cousin. We had heard about their situation. They had been living in another state but moved back to stay with her parents. His wife expressed her fears as a spouse, caregiver, and mother. They had recently had a baby, and she was worried about caring for her husband, their older son, and the newborn. She felt scared and overwhelmed, as anyone would who found themselves in this situation. Again, the only thing we could offer was to pray for them and provide support and assistance whenever they needed something; that small gesture made a significant difference.

Each person shared their hardships, fears, frustrations, and hopes while asking one another questions. When everyone had shared, and the meeting was winding down, we prayed that God would bless each person who attended. Then we served the cookies. Conversations continued, and tears were replaced by laughter. The meeting came to a close. Participants expressed what the evening had meant to them, and almost all mentioned feeling significantly better. We felt better, too, though, mainly because it was over! Mom was wonderful in connecting with the other patients and caregivers; she offered support and encouragement to everyone. *I was so proud of her!*

As the people were slowly leaving, the last gentleman to exit closed the door behind him, then opened it again and asked, "What time do we meet next week?" Next

Diana Thomi at one of early support groups of Victory in the Valley

week wasn't on our calendar! Surprised, Mom looked at me and said, "If you come back next week, we'll have one more meeting." That was our long-term plan. After he closed the door again, Mom turned to me and said, "Can you believe it? I didn't know what to say! Now we have to do this again. But I'm so happy they felt like they received help."

We didn't even have time to share our thoughts about this meeting before we had to think about the next one! We cleaned up the leftover cookies, I gave Mom a hug, and we talked about the people who attended. I asked

Mom how she felt physically, and she replied that she was energized and that the meeting had benefited her, too.

By the next meeting, we had run out of space in our home. One of the ladies who attended the support meetings invited us to her much larger home in the College Hill area of Wichita. This dear lady had participated in a women's tea at her church, where all the ladies were served on china plates and crystal, except her. She was served on paper plates and in a paper cup because the other women were afraid they might "catch" cancer. In the early 1980s, people didn't discuss cancer; they just whispered about you if you had it.

Soon, we found ourselves running *out of space* in this woman's larger home. A neighborhood church heard about our need for a meeting place from some of its members and generously opened the church parlor for our use at no cost.

The group continued to grow from the ten or fifteen cancer patients and caregivers who attended the first meeting to the forty or fifty individuals coming to the meetings at the church. There were new attendees at each meeting, and the numbers kept increasing. Oncologists, radiation doctors, nurses, and other healthcare professionals began speaking at our meetings and referring their patients to us. How did this happen?

In 1983, we continued meeting at the church, welcoming new cancer patients and their family members to the support meetings. At one such gathering, we encountered two new ladies- an older woman with cancer accompanied by a younger lady- both of whom appeared somewhat nervous about attending. We began the sharing time and mentioned that if anyone felt hesitant to share, we would appreciate it if they could at least tell us their names. As I observed the younger, beautiful lady, I noticed she had a "deer in the headlights" look and was clearly uncomfortable about sharing. Eventually, it was their turn. The older woman expressed that she had been battling cancer for some time and wanted to attend the meeting to learn more about cancer and its treatments. She also mentioned that their husbands worked together and that she didn't want to come alone.

The young woman introduced herself as Linda Mae Richardson, stating that she had melanoma with 50 malignant lymph nodes. At 32 years old, she was the mother of two small boys. She was receiving treatment at MD Anderson Cancer Center in Houston. When she asked her doctor about the odds of beating the cancer, he informed her that she had a 5 percent chance of living for one year. However, he also shared something that I remember as if it were yesterday: he told her that she was not a statistic and said,

## "Today, we are all one hundred percent alive, so don't forget to LIVE!"

He reminded her that we all need to focus on living each day to the *fullest* and *not* to waste it!

We concluded the meeting with a prayer and began to visit with the new attendees. I felt deeply saddened about Linda. Her prognosis was grim, and she was so young. I told her I was grateful she had opened up to us, and she replied, "After I heard the others share, I realized that they felt many of the same things I feel, and it made it easier to talk about." We invited her to the next meeting, and she expressed her thanks but didn't commit.

In my nursing experience, I had never known anyone who survived with Linda's diagnosis and the extensive spread of cancer. I felt sad that someone so young, with two small children, was facing such hardship, and I said a prayer for her whenever God brought her to mind. We were thrilled to see her the following week at the next support meeting. It marked the beginning of a long and wonderful friendship. We witnessed her progress during her treatments and were amazed by the insights she shared to help others living with cancer. She began to share hopeful and encouraging comments with others, even while going through her own challenging journey of leaving her family every month to travel six hundred miles to Houston for treatment. She mentioned that she had learned to focus on the blessings she had instead of the difficulties. She noted that when we feel down, we need to reach out and encourage someone else. Helping another person can benefit you as well as them. She reached out to others and began to express her thoughts in the form of encouraging poems.

Participating in a support group is a valuable way for members to help and encourage one another while also receiving encouragement in return. We considered the idea of becoming a non-profit and began to realize that as long as people kept coming, we could continue to exist for a while.

Some of the questions raised at the support group meetings highlighted the lack of information provided to cancer patients, or at least the lack of understanding about their diseases. The patients who attended came from various socioeconomic backgrounds. Some were educators, professionals, and businesspeople, while others were less educated and felt intimidated about asking their doctors questions. All were welcomed and treated with love and respect, but I confess it was hard not to giggle when some mispronounced the type of cancer they had. One kind gentleman said he had cancer in his "prospect gland, " and another said she had cancer in her "pantry." However, we didn't smile or laugh because they shared the same questions, fears, and misunderstandings as others in the room. Cancer is a great leveler!

Another lady coped with her cancer by sharing a humorous incident. She recounted a Saturday when she and several neighbors were doing yard work. She had a breast prosthesis, and as she leaned over to pick up some trash, her prosthetic fell out, and her dog grabbed it and took off running. She started to chase him, yelling to the neighbors, "Stop my dog! He has my boob in his mouth!" If that doesn't get attention, nothing will! Everyone, including her, had a good laugh.

# 6

As time went on, some attendees suggested that we file with our state to become a nonprofit organization, as they wanted to make donations for items such as refreshments at meetings, flowers for hospitalized group members, and similar needs.

There were many requirements for becoming a nonprofit organization. Since we had several attorneys in our family, we consulted one for guidance. My cousin, Craig Shultz, agreed to help us organize and file with the state as a 501(c) (3) organization. We needed officers, but that was easy! Mom served as President, I was Vice President, and our nurse friend, Charlene Jantz, became Secretary/Treasurer. However, before we could meet all the requirements, we needed a name.

Meanwhile, Mom continued her treatments, and as she met other cancer patients, she took the opportunity to invite them and their caregivers to the meetings.

Mom continued her daily habit of reading Scripture and praying, and she came across an article in *Streams in the Desert* based on 1 Kings 20:23-30. The devotional from this passage described how the Israelites and the Syrians were fighting each other in the hills. The Syrians were losing, so their king said, "The God of Israel is a God of mountains and not a God of valleys; therefore has he prevailed against us; but if we should fight against them in the plain, verily we shall prevail against them" (Brenton Septuagint). Following the king's command, they moved the battle to the valley, and once again, the Israelites won. The devotional concluded with, "Our God is God of the Hills *and* the Valleys!"

The story expressed how Mom felt during her cancer journey. It was a "valley" time in her life. Not only was the diagnosis frightening, as she was told she only had a short time to live, but she felt as though she was being pushed over the edge of life into a valley of fear, frustration, and apprehension. During this time, she spent much time in prayer and Bible study. Like many other patients, she questioned, "Why me? What have I done to deserve this? Why has God allowed this to happen to me?" Her answers unfolded in the Scriptures, as the Syrians claimed that God was God of the hills, but they could overcome Israel in the valley because that was a place of weakness and vulnerability for them. Mom could relate, as she felt vulnerable and physically very weak and tired. She found encouragement as she read how Israel defeated and destroyed the Syrians because

God is not only the God of the hills but also of the valleys. He is GOD!

I believe we can all relate to the fact that everyone goes through challenging times in life, especially during cancer. In the valleys, we often feel afraid and alone. However, when we know God and remember that *He* is the God of both the hills **and** *the valleys*, we can walk through the tough times in life with HIM. This thought inspired the name of our nonprofit organization, "**Victory in the Valley.**"

Many people also believe our name originated from Psalm 23 ("Yea, though I walk through the valley of the shadow of death"[v.4]). However, I have learned that the actual location of the battle in 1 Kings 20:23-30 in Israel resembles a ravine more than a valley, with high, steep sides and a narrow, treacherous floor filled with snakes, dangerous animals, large boulders, and rugged terrain. When you find yourself in this ravine, numerous shadows obscure your view of potential dangers ahead. It is the unknowns and changes that complicate navigation. These are the shadows: the shadows of fear, anger, anxiety, hopelessness, and confusion, alongside other negative emotions we may face. They represent the "shadows of death." The ravine's sides are exceptionally high, making it impossible to simply climb out. The only way out of the valley is to move *through it*.

That's how it is with cancer. We would love to run away, deny we have it, or find some other way to escape, but we can't! We must go *through it*. But how wonderful and amazing it is that when we know the Shepherd, we are never alone! He is there to walk with us, sometimes carry us, and always lead us through the trial. He sees the dangers, the boulders, and knows our fears lurking in the shadows. What a comfort to know that whatever comes into our lives, we will never be alone because our Shepherd has promised never to leave us. He is always there, but most especially when we face such difficult times as this.

As I walked alongside Mom through her battle with cancer, I observed her approach each treatment, every fearful thought, and each doctor visit with calm confidence. I knew she was scared, yet I admired her attitude; even though she hated all of it, she focused on enduring whatever she needed to do to survive.

Throughout her life, she maintained a positive attitude and rarely complained. I admired her because not many people, including myself, could face a trial like cancer in that way. However, I experienced a multitude of emotions throughout her treatment.

Sometimes, being a nurse doesn't help. I knew I was overprotective, but I didn't care. I felt compelled to watch for complications, like infections when her blood counts were low. I watched her closely, like a hawk. I'm sure I smothered Mom many times, disguising it as "being concerned." Mom was gracious, but at times, she reminded me that she- not I- was still the mom. I would understand for a while and then back off a little.

For instance, when Mom was in the middle of her treatments, her brother was hospitalized, and she wanted to see him since he was not expected to recover. I told her that hospitals are full of germs, and she probably shouldn't visit him. Again, she reminded me that she was the mom. So, I drove her to the hospital to see him. Looking back, I'm so glad she visited him that day because it wasn't long before he passed away. I would have felt terrible if I had prevented her from that visit, which reminded me that I needed to be the daughter, not the nurse.

I realized that Mom was aware of her limitations and how she felt physically. She didn't need me to give her permission to do what she felt she could safely handle. Often, we see so clearly what we think the other person needs or what they should or shouldn't do. However, they know how they feel and what they can or cannot do, and we need to respect their feelings, even if we think we know best- unless, of course, it could pose a danger to them.

When Mom recognized that she needed rest, she took the time to do so. I learned to pay attention to her cues. Sometimes, when she wanted to lie down, I would sit beside her on the bed. It was quiet and calm, allowing us to have some of the best heart-to-heart talks, which I treasure to this day.

In May 1984, we filed with the state of Kansas as a nonprofit organization with an annual budget of $250 (after all, we had cookies to buy!); Victory in the Valley, Inc. was born! Little did we know what God had in store for this small group of cancer patients and for my mom, who had already spent most of her life helping others.

After becoming incorporated, Victory in the Valley began attracting attention within the community. The oncology doctors noticed our growth and started recognizing the new and much-needed services we provided for their patients at no charge. We frequently invited the doctors to speak to the support group, benefiting not only the patients but also the doctors, as it allowed them to get acquainted with us and observe our work in action. They began referring cancer patients to us for assistance with transportation to and from treatments, along with additional services, encouragement, support group meetings, and hope.

We continued to meet at the church, and our support group grew to an average of 50 to 80 patients and caregivers each week.

In 1986, KAKE-TV held a televised event recognizing ten volunteers from the community who were making a difference. It was titled "10 Who Care." Mom was chosen as one of the ten for founding Victory in the Valley, Inc. It was announced that Mom's long-term goal was to provide a lodging facility for out-of-town cancer patients receiving treatment in Wichita. People began to familiarize themselves with the name, and we started receiving donations toward the lodging project.

We were new, and no one clearly understood what we were with the name "Victory in the Valley." It made for interesting mail. We received letters addressed to: "Lily of the Valley," "Hidden Valley (they must have thought we made salad dressing!)," "Big Valley," and my favorite, "Victory in the Alley." Sometimes, that's how it felt!

# 7

In 1986, Mom had completed her treatments and was regaining her energy. She began volunteering in the oncology unit at the hospital, where she met cancer patients from all over the state seeking treatment. Since most radiation treatments are daily, some patients were fortunate enough to afford lodging in Wichita, but many others could not.

A young mother of five from western Kansas traveled to Wichita to see the doctors. Her husband drove her but had to return home to work and care for the children. They didn't have much money, so he found the cheapest lodging available: a low-rent room in a less-than-desirable part of downtown, where she placed a chair in front of the door for safety and stayed alone until her next treatment. The Radiation Center asked if we could help.

We arranged for one of Mom's friends to pick her up from Monday to Friday and take her to treatments. After she finished each day, the volunteer would stop at a fast-food restaurant drive-thru to get her something to eat, then take her back to her room, where she would stay by herself until the next day. Her husband and children tried to visit her as often as they could on the weekends. It's so sad when someone has to leave home, friends, and family to undergo treatment alone. She was very sweet and grateful, as she wouldn't have been able to receive treatment at all if we hadn't helped her. She and her husband were incredibly thankful to us for helping her *LIVE!*

Mom met another lady from western Kansas who was taking her husband to daily radiation treatments. Her husband was extremely weak and ill, so she made a bed in the back of their station wagon and drove him two hundred twenty miles each way from their home to Wichita, where he would receive his twenty-minute treatment. Afterward, she would drive back home the same day. His treatment was five days a week for up to six weeks. When asked why they drove back and forth that long distance for daily treatments, the wife said, "We don't have the money to stay in town and buy food." We provided gift cards to help with food and gasoline. Once again, the need for lodging for patients and caregivers was at the forefront of our hearts and minds.

We began to recognize the challenges others were experiencing. Enduring cancer treatment is difficult enough, and frequently, we concentrate solely on ourselves and the obstacles we face. However, if we look around, we see many individuals encountering far worse situations than we are. During that time, it helps us to be grateful amidst our storm.

There was a sense of urgency to explore the possibility of providing answers for those traveling long distances for treatment. While Mom visited patients in the hospital, the cancer treatment centers reached out to her with requests for help for other patients in need of assistance and lodging. During this time, we began exploring options to offer lodging for out-of-town cancer patients and families coming to Wichita for treatment.

We looked at a beautiful home for sale near the hospital and envisioned a "Ronald McDonald" type house for adults. Since it was located in a neighborhood, it required rezoning. Together with our attorney, several of us appeared before the city zoning board with our request. Many local neighbors also attended the meeting and voiced their opposition to our intended use of the house in their community, which led the zoning board to rule against us. We were extremely disappointed and wondered what God had in mind to meet this crucial need. Our fervent prayers continued.

A few days after the "10 Who Care" television event, Mom received a phone call from a gentleman who said his friend had a facility for sale that would be perfect for our needs. He had watched the "10 Who Care" story and asked us to come and look at the facility. He informed us that it was a fully furnished apartment complex, which would be an ideal arrangement for us. Mom thanked him but indicated that we would not be interested as it would likely be far more than we could afford. (After all, we only had a $250 annual budget!) Undeterred, he kept calling, which became a bit irritating. Finally, reluctantly, and mostly so he would stop calling, Mom asked if I would go with her to see it.

Diana & Lois receiving awards

We arrived at the facility and couldn't believe our eyes. It was beautiful. There were nineteen fully furnished apartments, including studios, one-bedroom, and two-bedroom apartments, along with a separate building that housed laundry facilities. The entire project was only five years old and in perfect condition. Each apartment was fully furnished and move-in ready! It was just a few blocks from the hospital and the Cancer Center of

Kansas. It would be perfect for our out-of-town patients. We were so excited for a moment, as it seemed better than we could have hoped for! Then we came to our senses and asked, "How much?" The answer caused the blood to drain from our faces. "It's $650,000." For a moment, we wondered how long it would take to pay that off with our budget of $250 a year. It would be impossible. I felt sick, and Mom said something like, "Oh, my lands! There is no way! Thank you so much for showing us, but we can't even begin to think about it."

The man who showed us the apartment complex was a friend of the property owner and attempted to explain how we could make it happen; however, we didn't hear a word he said. To us, it was over.

As part of our transformation into a nonprofit organization, we established a board of directors made up of business professionals, cancer survivors, and financial experts. We reached out to the board members, and they all agreed that it was an impossible task. After a brief discussion, we concluded our conversation about this project.

We were sad but continued to ask God to help us find the right place to serve these patients and families who had to go to an unfamiliar location to receive assistance with their cancer.

Mom continued to meet other cancer patients in the hospital. One of these patients, Jackie Doskocil, was also undergoing cancer treatment. Jackie and her husband, Larry, were wonderful Christian people interested in learning more about Victory in the Valley. Mom shared the possibility of the apartment complex with Jackie and asked her and Larry to pray about it. Jackie informed her husband about the project, and he called Mom for more information. He said, "I heard about this lodging project you want to pursue. I think it is a very worthwhile endeavor, so I will give you $100,000 from my foundation. I believe you should proceed." Mom called the board chairman and me with the news. She then contacted the owners of the apartment complex and explained what we planned to do if we were able to purchase the property. The owners replied, "We really believe in what you want to do, so we will reduce the price by $100,000." We were all overwhelmed with joy! How could this be? We received $200,000 in one day! We were speechless!

Larry & Jackie Doskocil - Early major donor couple who launched The Lodge

My cousin Pat, whom we visited in Chicago, also wished to help with this project and made a substantial donation. We were on our way! There was no doubt this was what God had planned. We were stunned!

We were blessed by the Doskocil family in many ways. As we got to know Jackie better, we witnessed how she faced her cancer. She shared her heart with us when she said, "I think, among other things, that when we are diagnosed with cancer, we learn to let go of the things that don't truly matter. We learn that what we buy, we will only keep for a little while; it is what we give away that we truly keep. Love is not just a feeling; love is a learned behavior, and love must involve action. I think that sometimes, in our society, we are permeated with the thought that we will wait until the feeling comes and then say, 'I'll do something.' The older I get and the more I listen and learn, the more convinced I am that we must act out of love and let the feelings come later. If we can find a way to meet a need, I believe one of life's highest callings is to meet that need. If we can serve our fellow man and those who are struggling- some of whom feel so alone- we must do it."

Although Jackie lost her battle on Earth, she lived by these words and touched many lives with hope and encouragement.

Mom continued to share information about the lodging project. One of the key board members was Ron

Johnson, our CPA, who also happened to be a friend of the apartment owner. Ron played a vital role in encouraging his friend to sell to Victory in the Valley at a lower price. He was a wonderful man who guided Victory in the Valley for many years while serving as our treasurer on the board of directors.

Our board members, who knew many business people in the community, began meeting with executives from major companies. They explained the project and inquired whether they would be interested in sponsoring an apartment. Others got involved, and we were amazed by our community's enthusiastic response. At that time, Wichita, Kansas, was known for its aircraft industry and is still referred to as the "Air Capital of the World" because Cessna, Beech, and Boeing manufactured their planes there. All of them contributed funds to sponsor an apartment, and a nameplate designating their sponsorship was placed on the door of the apartment they sponsored. As we watched in awe, everything started to fall into place; it was a miracle unfolding! Before long, we were in the lodging business! We officially named it Victory in the Valley Lodge, but referred to it as The Lodge. Once again, God proved that He is the God of the impossible!

Later, we applied for and received a matching grant from the Kansas Health Foundation. The Foundation agreed to match any funds we raised to help pay for The Lodge. Several businesses and foundations awarded us grants that the health foundation matched; consequently,

Lois standing outside the Victory Lodge

between the money we raised and the matching donation, we were able to completely pay off the loan. It was incredible!

Many special people came into our lives to be part of what God was doing through Victory in the Valley. By this time, a very special man named Britt Fulmer had become our chairman of the board. He had a great sense of humor and dressed impeccably, as he owned an exclusive menswear store. I will always remember our first Cancer Survivors Day Celebration. It was an outdoor event, and Britt served as the emcee, sitting on the stage. The event included the release of doves in honor of all cancer survivors. Britt wore his usual high-end clothing and shoes, and just as a dove flew over his head, it "let go," and the unsightly droppings landed on him. Taking it all in stride, Britt made a face of disgust and then started laughing. He used to say, "If that's the worst thing that happens to me, I'm good." (The rest of us went from apologizing to almost getting sick!)

Britt served as the Board Chairman for many years because we wouldn't let him resign. Each time his term ended, we simply rolled it over into the next term. Britt always served with his heart and made a lasting impact on everyone he met.

Britt Fulmer – Beloved, long-time, Board Chairman for Victory in the Valley

In times of discouragement or crisis, Britt would remain calm and remind us that God knew all the details and that He had never failed us. What a man of great faith and encouragement! After being diagnosed with cancer in the last stages, he was asked how he felt about his prognosis and the prospect of dying prematurely. True to Britt's faith in God, he answered: "Why would I want to stay here, except for my family, when I will get a new body and forever be with the One who loves me most?" He was always living his faith, serving as an encourager and an example of a life well-lived. He lost his battle with cancer but gained a heavenly home. We miss him dearly but will never forget him. He taught us so much through the way he lived his life. He never doubted his relationship with God and lived a life of faith, trust, and joy. Britt went home to be with the Lord on June 28, 2021. He openly shared his faith, and his homegoing service focused on how we can all join him in Heaven someday. What an incredible honor it was to serve alongside him for so many years.

Mom and our small staff began sharing information about our lodging assistance with various churches and community members. Many business people on our board knew others who might be interested in supporting The Lodge. They would schedule an appointment, and Mom and the board member would meet with anyone who expressed interest. Typically, the board member who had the contact would make the appointment call, after which

Mom, the board member, or the chairman would go to meet them and address their questions.

Since all the apartments had full kitchens, we began receiving gifts of groceries that filled the cupboards with food for the residents. As we collected donations of groceries, we also started an additional grocery pantry to assist local cancer patients and families undergoing treatment who were struggling financially. Cancer takes its toll in many areas, not only physically but also emotionally and financially.

One Christmas season, this became very clear to me. We received a referral from a doctor's office regarding a couple whose husband had cancer. They were struggling in every aspect, trying to provide for their five children for Christmas as well as meet their everyday needs. The dad had been unable to work for several months due to his cancer treatments. The mother had not worked outside the home but took a temporary job to bring in some income. We were blessed by the community and volunteers with many gifts, groceries, and meat items, and this family truly pulled at our heartstrings. We put together a generous box of groceries and gifts for each family member so the children would have at least one present to open on Christmas.

We asked the family if someone could pick up the gifts and groceries; if not, we would deliver them. They agreed to come. When the day arrived, the husband pulled up in a brand-new pickup truck, exited, and turned to activate his keyless entry. I met him at the door and introduced myself.

For a moment, I felt jealous and thought this family might be taking advantage of us, possibly not even in need. You see, I didn't even have keyless entry on *my* car!

A moment later, I sensed God telling me that I was judging and that it was not my place to do so. I experienced a quick attitude adjustment as the gentleman approached and thanked me. I asked how he was doing, and he replied, "You know when a man can't provide for his family, it's a terrible feeling. I can't do my job yet, but my boss allowed me to come back to run a few errands for the company so I could have a little money for Christmas. In fact, that's his new truck he lent me to get our groceries and gifts."

Imagine my shame upon reflecting on my judgmental attitude. Oh, what a lesson I will never forget! I was reminded that cancer affects both the rich and the poor, and even if someone drives an expensive car with keyless entry and lives in a fancy neighborhood, cancer remains the greatest equalizer. There is never room for judgment, but there is always room for helping and caring for those on their cancer journey!

The Lodge addressed real needs as we encountered patients and family members from across the state traveling to Wichita for treatment. We charged $25 per night for lodging, and if they were unable to pay that amount, we invited them to contribute whatever they could.

The stories were sad, and once again, we recognized that even in difficult times, others had to leave their homes, families, and even their pets to stay in the 'big city' for weeks on end.

One older lady was staying by herself in one of The Lodge's apartments, as she didn't have much family. Her husband had brought her to Wichita from a small Kansas town. He returned home to work and didn't visit often. When her treatment was finished, he NEVER returned to pick her up!

A family with several children traveled to Wichita from Dighton, KS, to see the pediatric oncologist, Dr. David Rosen. Their three-year-old daughter, Gracie, had been diagnosed with cancer in her right sinus and was facing long-term treatment. They needed a place to stay where the whole family of five could be together, so they were referred to us. They were a wonderful Christian family and quickly became part of our own. Gracie was doing well, but the treatments were very hard on her. The family was very musical; they would sing for us, the other cancer patients, or at our support group meetings, bringing joy and encouragement even amid their struggles.

Victory Kids: Gracie (cancer patient, age 4, family utilized Victory in the Valley Lodge)

One day, they called us and asked if we could come to the hospital. Gracie had taken a turn for the worse, and her blood count was so low that they weren't sure she was going to live. Of course, we immediately went to the hospital, where we stood with the family at her bedside and prayed for the frail little body lying on the bed. We asked God to bring healing and strength back to this sweet girl who had captured our hearts. The next day, we received a call saying she was doing better and was out of danger. Today, she is a young adult who continues to sew, quilt, and cook at a camp in Oklahoma. She uses her talents to serve others and understands the importance of not dwelling on the past and everything she went through, using her experiences to bless others.

Another couple who stayed with us traveled to Kansas from Arizona for the Christmas holidays. The husband, Richard, became ill and was admitted to a local hospital in a small western Kansas town. Due to the seriousness of his diagnosis, he was later transferred to a hospital in Wichita, where he underwent surgery for a malignant brain tumor. When Richard was discharged from the hospital, the couple needed a place to stay, and their doctor recommended Victory in the Valley Lodge. They stayed for eight weeks while he received radiation treatment. Richard was a fascinating man; he worked on the space shuttle as Chief of Program Planning and was involved in nuclear research. He contributed to the Viking Lander that went to Mars and many other missile projects. Away from home during a crisis and throughout the Christmas season, they found care and friendship at The Lodge that lasted a lifetime. Unfortunately, he has passed, but his wife continues to support Victory in the Valley with donations. What an honor it is to serve others in the most challenging times.

# Quotes and Thank Yous from Cancer Patients & Families

"Victory in the Valley has been a very special place for me during my journey with cancer. I can't tell you how wonderful the Hospitality Centre's existence was during the first few months of my treatment. Your staff and their kindness, encouragement, and laughter were truly key to my recovery."

―――――――

"I wanted to send a note to thank you for all you do! I have recently come to realize how blessed Kansas is to have a group like you in existence, and I wanted to share my experience with you. At age 24, when I was diagnosed with cancer, there were very few people my age that I knew of who had been cancer patients…later, I found out that my cancer had returned and I started traveling to Denver, CO, for treatment. I looked for something similar to Victory in the Valley and there were no services available. I realized what a gift you are to us! Thank you for all you do, you bless our lives so much!"

"Of all the dark times which cancer brought into our lives, Victory in the Valley was the bright spot."

<hr />

"Thank you, Victory in the Valley, for helping my son have a ride to receive his cancer treatments. Our son died in March. Please let the drivers know how much we appreciated their help."

<hr />

"Special note must be made of Victory in the Valley, a support organization that provides, without cost, whatever it can to make life easier for a cancer patient and their primary caregiver. Wigs, turbans, prostheses, overnight accommodations for out-of-town patients and caregivers, a place of comfort to wait in between the lab work and the doctor or chemo, snacks, someone who has been through your experience to talk to (if you wish), the list is too extensive to list all the ways they support those affected. Not all of these items were needed for us, but it gives you an idea of the scope of what they do. Their constant support was of immeasurable value to us, and we thank them."

<hr />

"Words don't seem adequate to express our appreciation for all the love, support and prayers for our mother. None of us will ever look at a teddy bear without thinking of Victory in the Valley and our mother."

―――――

"I received a wig from you this past July before I started chemo. I have since finished my treatments and am on the road to recovery. I have received so many compliments on my wig, and I am so thankful for you every day. Thanks for being there for me, and God bless you all."

―――――

"What you have done for me no words can express. I've had breast cancer twice and now I am a survivor. My faith in God, and your love, has gotten me through some rough times. I am now cancer free and loving every breath of my life. All things are possible with God."

―――――

"Diana- your mom visited us in the hospital when our son was first diagnosed. She gave us hope and encouragement with such grace. She was an exceptional angel from God here on this earth. A woman beautiful in so many caring ways. You were fortunate to have had her so many years and to be her daughter. Our thanks to you and your family for all you have done for cancer patients in Kansas. Peace be with you."

# 8

Linda Mae Richardson, as you may remember from the chapter about the support group, was a young woman diagnosed with fifty malignant lymph nodes due to melanoma. She attended the early support group meeting with a friend. Her doctors at MD Anderson in Houston, TX, informed her that she had a 5% chance of surviving for a year. However, Linda was nothing short of a miracle. She lived for forty years cancer-free after her diagnosis and was grateful for every day she was blessed with. She referred to these as "bonus days" and heeded her doctor's words that we are all 100 % alive...so she fully lived each one!

Linda shared her cancer experience with us. She mentioned that she had always had many moles on her body and enjoyed being in the sun, playing tennis, swimming, and staying active. One day, she noticed a lump in her neck that seemed to be growing larger, and after some time, she thought it best to have it checked. She visited her doctor, who examined it and referred her to an oncologist in town. After seeing the specialist, he expressed significant concern about that specific area in her neck. She informed him about her numerous moles, prompting him to suggest some testing and advising her to schedule an appointment later to receive the results.

Linda didn't care for this particular doctor, but she was frightened, so she felt she had no choice after coming this far in the process. On the day she returned for the results, she sat in the waiting room with another patient who was crying. After a short time, Linda reached out to the woman, who told her that the doctor was moving out of town and that she was upset because she thought he was wonderful. Since Linda didn't care for him at all, she was glad he was leaving. She kept the appointment for the results and was informed that the tests showed she had melanoma. Since the doctor was moving, she would need to go somewhere else for further follow-up. He felt the situation was serious and advised her to go to MD Anderson Cancer Center in Houston, TX, to see a specialist for her type of cancer. Since there was no physician in Wichita who specialized in her form of cancer, he advised her to schedule an appointment as soon as possible. He expressed that he was very concerned. Naturally, she was frightened, as she had two little boys at home and had hoped she was not facing cancer, but each day, the area on her neck seemed to be getting larger.

Even with the unsettling news, she was relieved that she wouldn't have to see this doctor again because she wasn't fond of his abrupt manner and lacked confidence in him. She learned a valuable lesson that day: not everyone connects with a doctor in the same way, but it's essential to have a doctor you trust who communicates effectively with you. The journey you're on is challenging, and you need to have confidence in who is guiding you. A doctor might be highly regarded, but if you're hesitant to ask questions or express your feelings, it undermines your confidence. We are all unique and require different types of support. Perhaps you prefer to hear the facts and move on, or maybe you need more detailed explanations and the chance to ask questions to gain reassurance and the strength to follow their recommendations. Remember, the doctor is there for you; you should feel they are also collaborating with you.

Linda and her husband, Tom, traveled to Houston to see the specialist. He recommended that she begin treatment immediately, as the melanoma was spreading quickly. Thus began her monthly trips to MD Anderson for treatment. Often, she went alone, but it was difficult for Linda to face the treatment and the resulting nausea by herself. Sometimes, her parents could accompany her, and at other times, Tom could go. Linda's sister cared for their boys when both parents were away. However, as much as he wished to be there with her, Tom often had to stay home and work to avoid losing their insurance coverage. But God was with her in the form of friends from their church in Wichita. The family had relocated to Houston, and when they learned about Linda's situation, they invited her to stay with them whenever she had to come alone for treatment. They graciously loaned her their car so she could drive to MD Anderson. They were a wonderful blessing at just the right moment, reminding us that no matter what we go through, God is with us and goes before us to prepare the way. What a blessing and gift from God in the hearts of His children!

After several years of treatments, surgeries, and tests, Linda was considered to be in remission. She continued to return for follow-ups for a few years. During those years of treatment and testing, Linda utilized her experiences and insights to write hundreds of poems and materials that were meant to bless others on their cancer journey.

Linda Mae Richardson

After that early group meeting, Linda remained actively involved with Victory in the Valley. As a valuable volunteer, she shared her experiences with cancer by visiting patients in hospitals and informing others about Victory in the Valley. Soon, she began helping to lead support groups and writing poems to encourage other cancer patients and their families. Although she continued to go to MD Anderson for checkups, she was no longer undergoing treatment.

After we purchased The Lodge, our staff mainly consisted of Mom, the two front office ladies who managed the lodging business, and two housekeepers. Mom, who had previously managed multiple Montgomery Ward stores in various states, was excellent at business management. However, she was still recovering from her final, year-long treatment for cancer and was growing weary. In 1987, I was able to leave my nursing job at the hospital to help Mom with the additional growth, fundraising activities, and speaking requests.

Maintaining our lodging needs, including finances, remained a constant concern. We soon sought a part-time secretary to join our staff and considered Linda. She had been a secretary years ago before choosing to stay home with her two young boys. However, the boys were older now and didn't require her to be at home. We asked if she would be interested in working with us part-time.

She joined our team and worked part-time for one week. In that brief period, we realized how valuable she was- both for her ability to communicate with cancer patients due to her own experience with cancer and for her numerous secretarial skills. She remarked that it was the shortest part-time job she ever had; after one week, we asked her to become full-time!

Linda loved working at Victory in the Valley because it felt less like a job and more like a place where she could minister to those who walked through the doors. She could say just the right things to others, having walked that journey herself and always giving credit to the Lord for His grace in allowing her to see her sons grow up, marry, and enjoy her wonderful grandchildren. She and Tom spent almost every weekend taking care of them and watching them grow. It was all those experiences that made her think that during her battle with cancer, she wouldn't get to enjoy them.

As a secretary, Linda helped carry the load in several areas. Additionally, God had given her the gift of writing, and her poems continue to bless many who are starting their cancer journeys. Over time, her poems were requested by MD Anderson, Mayo Clinic, Memorial Sloan-Kettering Cancer Center, and several other major cancer centers. She wrote over 500 poems about life and the cancer experience, which have been sent throughout the United States and five foreign countries. She also began leading our cancer support groups. In addition to writing poems, she authored support group discussion notes on nearly every topic related to cancer, sending these notes to all our support group chapters in Kansas each month. Though now in heaven, she continues to live on at Victory in the Valley, where we still send her monthly notes to all of our support groups throughout the state.

Linda was a wonderful friend who always thought of others before herself. She regarded Mom as her "other mother." The three of us took many work trips together to establish a new support group outside Wichita. She nominated Mom for various awards and consistently promoted Victory in the Valley during television interviews and newspaper articles. Thanks to Linda's advocacy, we were honored to be among the recipients of President Bush's Points of Light Award.

Because of Linda's promotion, we won many local awards. However, when we attempted to nominate Linda for an award, she refused to accept it. We tried to compile her poems into a book to sell or even give away to patients, but she declined to allow us. She preferred that they be distributed individually to those in need and did not want credit. She was a caring friend to others, deeply concerned about those who were struggling. She shared her wisdom from personal experiences while informing others about the services offered by Victory in the Valley.

We were incredibly blessed to have her on staff for over thirty-six years. She was one of the greatest influences contributing to the success of Victory in the Valley, as well as to Mom and me personally. She served faithfully until her death in February 2020. At the age of seventy-two, she unexpectedly went to her heavenly home to be with the One she always wanted to thank and honor with her life. Those of us who knew her will never forget how she lived her life and used her talents to bless and help others. Her words continue to support and encourage cancer patients and their families every day.

# 9

As Victory in the Valley expanded its outreach, we became increasingly aware that our small staff could no longer accomplish what was necessary to serve the hundreds of cancer patients we were seeing. We had an informal group of volunteers who were doing an excellent job of helping, but we wanted to formalize our volunteer opportunities in a more organized manner. This way, the volunteers could choose the areas they felt comfortable and enjoyed working in.

In 1989, we formed the Victory in the Valley Volunteer Association and selected Betty Nell Stephan, also a cancer survivor, as the Association President. At that time, her husband, Robert Stephan, was the Attorney General of Kansas. Betty Nell was a kind, bubbly, outgoing woman with a warm smile who loved people. No one was a stranger to her, and she understood what cancer patients and their caregivers were experiencing because she had walked that path with her husband.

The volunteer association enabled us to "spread the joy" of serving by providing volunteers wherever needed. Gradually, new individuals who wanted to join in serving cancer patients began to arrive. Over the years, we grew to 287 volunteers engaged in various activities: visiting hospitals and The Lodge, sewing, cooking, leading support groups, and transporting patients to treatment.

There was a small house next to our facility that was donated to Victory in the Valley. After a few renovations, the volunteers transformed it into a store and collected donations to sell, helping to cover cancer patients' needs. Volunteers took turns managing the store, which provided a fun way to connect with one another while serving cancer patients and members of the community. All proceeds from the sales were used to support our services.

# 10

One of Victory in the Valley's strengths was and continues to be its ability to respond to the unmet needs of cancer patients in our community and state.

We heard about cancer patients who couldn't keep their appointments for oncology treatments due to a lack of transportation or because they lived alone and were unable to drive themselves due to side effects. The number of those needing reliable transportation to and from oncology treatments seemed to continue to grow.

In 1988, we presented this need to our board, who responded enthusiastically. This was a program we needed to implement. Our goal was not only to offer transportation but also to hire drivers who had experienced cancer to ensure that each patient received understanding and encouragement from someone who had shared a similar journey. The rides became "mini support groups" for those just beginning their journey and were far more uplifting than an Uber driver!

We sent a grant request to the Fred and Mary Koch Foundation and were thrilled to receive a letter notifying us that our request was approved. We used the grant money to purchase a van and hire two drivers, both of whom were either cancer survivors or caregivers. The rides were always free, but we made one request of those receiving them: we asked the patients to fill out a "thank you" card, which we would forward to the Koch Foundation in appreciation for the grant that provided the vehicle they were riding in. The patients were more than willing to include a note, and we loved being able to send the notes from those who needed the services most.

One woman wrote, "Dear Mr. and Mrs. Koch, I just wanted to thank you for saving my life! If you hadn't provided a ride to treatment, I probably would have died. Now my cancer is responding, and I'm going to live!"

I can only imagine how much the Koch family enjoyed knowing they made a difference in so many lives in our community!

Over the years, numerous vans have been donated by various companies and individuals to support this important outreach, including foundations from Spirit Aerosystems, Cessna, John and Martha Crum, The Hedrick Foundation, and the family of Sam Davidson.

Each donation has significantly impacted the lives of cancer patients by providing vehicles for transportation.

One of the patients we were privileged to transport was a gentleman living in a rundown house in a very poor part of town. It was clear that he was struggling both financially and physically. On the first day our driver picked him up, he explained that he could not pay for the ride. We reassured him that it was our joy to help him receive his treatment, and we did not want him to worry about payment.

His treatments were five days a week for several weeks. Each day, he told the driver that he wanted to give us some money. They had the same conversation every time: that we didn't want any money, that we were happy to help. Finally, the day of his last treatment arrived. Expecting to have the same conversation, the gentleman thanked the driver for all the rides and asked him to hold out his hand. Out of respect, the driver complied, and the gentleman dropped thirty-seven cents into his hand and said, "I wish it was more, but that's all the money I have!" With tears in his eyes, the driver brought the thirty-seven cents to the office and told us that the gentleman wanted it to help with gas for the transportation program.

How humbling, and what an honor!

Our driver, George, assisting patient to treatment

It has been nearly thirty years since we began offering this free service to individuals who otherwise would not have access to care due to transportation difficulties. We averaged over twenty thousand miles driven each year across the city, transporting patients to their treatments and safely returning them home.

## Finding a "listening ear" from someone who has been there and who understands with their heart is priceless!

# 11

In 1990, President George H.W. Bush initiated the creation of the Daily Points of Light, a private, non-profit organization designed to promote volunteerism. Now simply called Points of Light, its purpose has always been and continues to encourage volunteerism and community service. It is recognized as the world's largest organization dedicated to volunteer service. While Bush was president, he honored certain individuals and organizations with the Daily Point of Light Award to recognize their exemplary service, which had a positive and transformative impact on others.

In 1991, things were going well for our organization, and we were especially thrilled that oncologists were referring cancer patients and their families to Victory in the Valley. We had started a daytime support group in addition to the evening group we had initially launched. Both groups were growing and quietly serving those with cancer and their caregivers. Unbeknownst to us, Linda had nominated us that year for President Bush's

Daily Point of Light Award, which honors individuals who serve others in their communities.

One day, as Mom, Linda, and I were quietly working in our office (which used to be an apartment in The Lodge), the phone rang. A voice on the other end said, "Hello, this is the White House calling. I would like to speak to someone in the Victory in the Valley administration." I answered the call and thought, "Okay, who is this really?" assuming it was a joke. For the second time since this journey began, I could hardly find my voice and merely said, "Seriously?" I was genuinely at a loss for words (which didn't happen very often). After confirming that the caller was indeed from the White House in Washington, DC, she informed me that we had been nominated as one of President George H.W. Bush's Daily Point of Light recipients *and* that we had been chosen! I almost dropped the phone but instead handed it to Mom, who was eager to hear what I was so excited about. As the lady from the White House repeated to my mother what she had conveyed to me, Mom's eyes widened, and a huge smile spread across her face. She jumped up and down a couple of times before hanging up. We couldn't believe it was true. What an amazing opportunity to celebrate! We were in disbelief, but we had been named the "471st Daily Point of Light" *by President H.W. Bush!*

We later received a letter from the President confirming that it was true.

Points of Light: Diana & Lois received medals from President Bush

A few weeks later, we received a letter informing us of a celebration for the Points of Light recipients at Disney World in Florida, and we were invited as guests of Disney. They would fly us to Orlando at their expense, and we would stay free of charge at one of the Disney properties. We would have full access to everything Disney offers as their guests. When the volunteers and board of directors heard the news, they were thrilled by the honor. I wish we could have taken everyone who contributed to the organization, but all were kind and celebrated with us. The local newspaper interviewed us about the honor and once again shared the story of Victory in the Valley and all the services we provide. It was a lifetime gift, and we were proud to represent everyone involved in Victory in the Valley.

The day finally arrived when Mom, Linda, and I boarded the plane headed to Florida. We received special badges that allowed us to enjoy all the benefits of the park, including food and activities. If we wanted to go on a ride, we stood in line with everyone until someone came to usher us to the front so we wouldn't have to wait. We had never felt so special and appreciated!

The Points of Light Award ceremony took place outdoors in a stadium, and Mom was ushered to the stage where she sat with the other recipients of the Points of Light Award, right behind the President! Soon, she was asked to give up her seat for a Secret Service agent, which, although she understood, didn't make her very happy. A beautiful gospel choir provided music; Lee Greenwood sang "God Bless the USA," and a large number of doves were released in our honor. We were all given medals and then led to a spacious dining area for lunch with President and Mrs. Bush. The President then spoke, and we enjoyed a wonderful luncheon. It was rumored that they flew in the White House china for our meal.

Later, Mom and I had the opportunity to speak personally and shake hands with the President and the First Lady! Only two representatives were allowed to attend, so unfortunately, Linda had to miss this part of the day, but she graciously enjoyed listening to us share everything that had happened. It was an incredible honor to represent all the staff and volunteers who made Victory in the Valley a tremendous success!

Several months later, President Bush came to Kansas City and invited us, as Point of Light recipients, to meet him. Selfishly, we wanted to attend and were excited to greet him at the airport and tour Air Force One. However, we felt we should let others enjoy this special occasion, so we asked our president of volunteers and The Lodge housekeeping manager to attend on our behalf. They met the president and represented everyone involved in the work of Victory in the Valley. For them, it was also a once-in-a-lifetime experience.

# 12

The monthly expenses for maintaining nineteen fully furnished apartments at The Lodge, which were almost always occupied, were substantial. During a board meeting in early 1992, it was suggested that we consider a fundraiser to help cover the ongoing expenses.

One of our board members mentioned that, given Wichita's early history, we might consider starting a race competition between the east and west sides of town. Historically, Wichita consisted of two distinct sections divided by the river. In the early days, the west side was home to cattle drives, saloons, and entertainment areas, while the east side boasted better shops and businesses, as well as the residences of doctors, lawyers, and other professionals. Ideas flowed during our board meeting, and by the end of the session, a tentative plan had taken shape. After much planning and preparation, the First Annual East vs. West Walk/Run was held in September 1992.

To maintain neutrality, the event took place at the Old Towne Farm and Art Market Plaza, located in the center of town. This inaugural event was held on Sunday evening of Labor Day weekend, with local restaurants generously donating food. An experienced event planner, Barbara Yarnell, volunteered to organize the occasion at no cost, which was a blessing since we were unsure how to proceed. She reached out to sponsors, arranged for the printing of posters and registrations, and obtained the necessary permissions. She ordered t-shirts in two colors for participants (one color for the east side and another for the west side). She also contacted local television and news media, which promoted the event. We invited two local celebrities to serve as the East and West team captains to enhance the competition and encourage participation from both sides of town.

There was something for everyone, including a 5K run, a 2K walk, and a kids' run. Equally significant was the Cancer Survivors Walk, which honored and highlighted individuals who had been diagnosed with cancer at any point in their lives, whether recently or long ago.

Today, anyone diagnosed with cancer is considered a survivor, as they continue to live despite the illness. The race event takes place annually, and although it has been modified, we maintain the Cancer Survivors Stroll, for they deserve support and honor not just once a year but every day! In May 2024, we completed the 32nd East Meets West Walk for Victory. This event remains our organization's main source of income, with all proceeds going towards funding our free services for cancer patients.

East/West Race – fundraiser for Victory in the Valley

# 13

Understanding that cancer can affect even young individuals, we developed a program for children with cancer. Our goal was to assist the entire family when a child was diagnosed. Often, when a child receives a cancer diagnosis, siblings, regardless of age, face challenges as the focus shifts to the sick child. Frequently, the ill child is showered with gifts from caring family and friends, while the healthy siblings may be overlooked. Since the whole family is experiencing a crisis, each member requires support and understanding. Therefore, we collaborated with pediatric oncologists and other professionals to offer assistance to parents and provide enjoyable activities for children, allowing them to experience a sense of normalcy while their parents connected with others facing similar situations. Parents could also enjoy watching their kids enjoy some normalcy and fun!

One of the most popular activities we had was the family "Victory Weekend." Throughout the weekend, there were games and various fun activities. The kids enjoyed swimming and crafting while the parents gathered to share their struggles and listen to speakers discussing topics such as how to help their child eat during chemotherapy and how to navigate sibling dynamics.

The weekend brought a shaving cream fight. Everyone joined in on this fun activity, including the pediatric oncologist- nothing beats spraying your doctor with shaving cream! You can only imagine over thirty kids running around like little white ghosts, daring to spray their parents and volunteers with the frothy foam. Once it concluded, the local fire department arrived with hoses to spray everyone down.

Victory Kids' Program: Shaving cream fight

One of the kids in our "Kids' Cancer Program" was a little boy named JC, diagnosed with leukemia at the age of two. He was "Mr. Personality," and everyone loved him. We all learned so much from him; he never lost his smile or complained about his situation.

He faced chemotherapy like a champ, and after months of treatment, he went into remission.

The pediatric oncologist, along with his parents and everyone who knew him, rejoiced when his counts stabilized. Then, sadly, after it seemed things were improving, he would relapse and have to begin treatment again. This was his life.

JC was a bundle of fun. He was always up for anything, whether he was picking his nose while sitting on Santa's lap at the Victory in the Valley Kids' Christmas party or meeting the famous Globetrotters. He was always laughing and full of joy!

He seemed to have an adult perspective on his cancer and its related challenges. Children dealing with cancer often show a level of maturity that many adults lack. Such was the case with JC. He went through periods of remission followed by relapse. His parents took him to major cancer centers across the United States until, finally, at the age of thirteen, there were no treatments, experimental or otherwise, left to explore.

Victory Kids' Program: JC on Santa's lap

JC was in the hospital when his uncle, a pastor, came to visit him. It was spring. As they chatted, JC started sharing all his summer plans with his uncle. He wanted to go deep-sea fishing, travel, and do many other activities. Then he told his uncle which classes he planned to take in school in the fall, although they both knew that unless there was a miracle, JC would not get to go fishing or attend school.

He died shortly after that. At his funeral, his uncle shared how JC had lived his short life to the fullest. He remarked that JC was aware he was dying, yet he *continued* living. His uncle captured his attitude by describing him as "casting anchors into the future" while also preparing for death.

On JC's playlist, there were many songs about heaven that filled the hours, and he listened to them frequently. I'm sure he found hope and comfort each time he heard them. His mother read the daily devotional book, Jesus Calling (Sarah Young, c2004), in which JC had written many notes to her, often sharing his thoughts on the pages, such as, "Mom, you need to remember this!" He let her know that he was okay and that he knew where he was going. What a comfort! JC touched all our lives with his wisdom and taught us how to live and prepare for death. He taught us that it's not always the *LENGTH* of our days that matters, but rather *HOW* we live them.

In 2018, Linda Mae Richardson wrote the following poem to honor JC and celebrate a life well-lived. The poem not only honors JC but also serves as a foundation for how Linda faced her battle with cancer. Time and again, she found the strength to continue her difficult fight against melanoma by relying on her relationship with God and the comforting words found in the Psalms.

No matter the storms we face in life, we all need anchors, and we can draw strength from the words of Scripture. It was this verse from Psalms, along with the words of JC's uncle, that inspired this poem by Linda.

He maketh the storm a calm so
that the waves thereof are still.
Psalm 107:29 (KJV)

## CASTING ANCHORS

By Linda Mae Richardson

When stormy seas have gathered round
When lightning strikes with loud resound
When tossed on waves of fearful thoughts
When seems my prayers have been forgot
When circumstances bring me down
I cast my anchors all around…
One for faith and hopes and dreams
A future filled with all good things.

For though the winds of fear shall come
And waves of doubt crash one by one…
"Tis God who calms the storms within…
With hope restored, I run to Him."
Then, knowing that God loves me so
I hear His words as wisdom grows…
"Come rest, my child-renew your strength,
I'll walk with you through journey's length."

# 14

After several years of serving children with cancer and their families, Wesley Medical Center established a children's hospital and continued many of the services and activities we had initiated. To support these services without duplicating them, we discontinued our program, and families are now served by Wesley Children's Hospital and other organizations.

Another favorite activity at the kids' parties, as well as during their chemotherapy treatments in the rooms, was visits from some special dogs.

The diagnosis and treatment of cancer can be among the most stressful times in life. Uncertainty about what to expect during treatment and beyond amplifies the stress surrounding the negative information you may have heard about cancer treatment.

Among all the programs offered by Victory in the Valley, one stands out as the most popular— "Canine Friends." Our program features certified therapy dogs

Canine friends and handlers

visiting cancer patients in the treatment rooms while they are actively receiving chemotherapy.

One of our volunteers had a certified therapy dog and asked the pediatric oncologist if it would be possible to visit children with cancer during their treatment. The pediatric oncologist welcomed the idea and said the handlers and dogs could visit anytime. In 2003, the Canine Friends program began.

The "Canine Friends" program requires therapy dogs to pass a rigorous test to ensure they are well-mannered guests. These dogs come in various shapes, sizes, colors, and breeds. Our therapy dogs have provided comfort to cancer patients and their families for many years. Handlers and their dogs offer furry visits at our Hospitality Centre, Victory House, cancer treatment rooms, and our support groups.

The "Canine Friends" program is dedicated to providing comfort and companionship by sharing dogs with cancer patients. In addition to loving and cuddling those who seek closeness, they entertain patients by performing tricks and often receive applause! Even the nurses occasionally slip the dogs a well-earned treat. This warm and fuzzy outreach is guaranteed to be a "bone-a-fide" success!

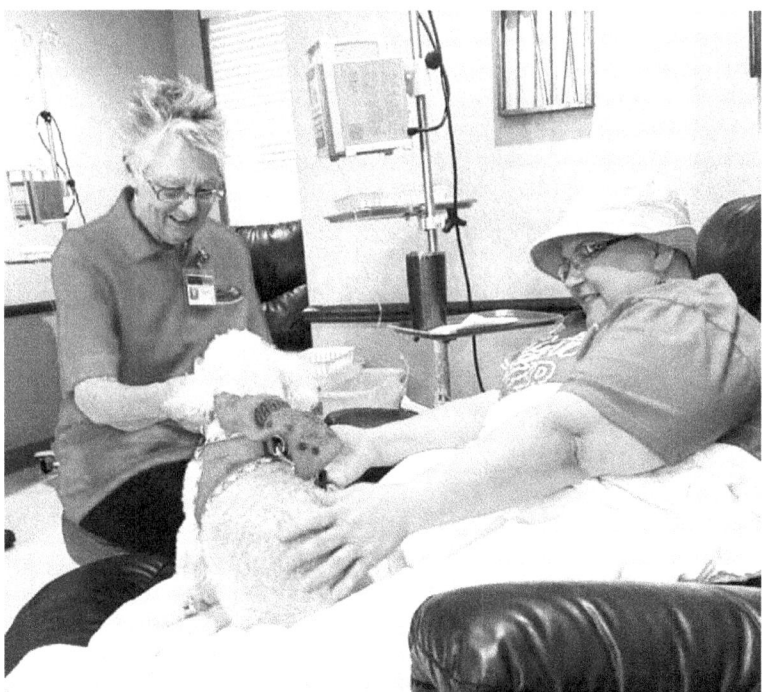

Canine friends visiting patient at the treatment center

# 15

When women lose their hair due to chemotherapy, they often experience a profound sense of loss. For women, hair is a significant part of their identity, and there is often a period of grieving as they confront the stark reality of their battle with cancer in the mirror. The reflection can look like a stranger staring back at them. It is one of the many changes that can occur, and can be very sad and depressing.

When Mom started losing her hair due to treatments, we contacted the American Cancer Society, which provided free wigs for cancer patients. They told us to come to their office, where we could browse through the wigs and find one that she liked. We made an appointment, and they took us to a small room filled with paper sacks of wigs that were neither clean nor styled. (I certainly do not mean to be unkind or ungrateful, but in fairness, they lacked space for anything more.) Mom examined a few wigs and then asked me, "Do I have to choose one of these?" I tried to hold back my tears as I replied, "No. Let's go. We will find just the right one for you."

We searched for places that sold wigs and found The Wig Shoppe in downtown Wichita. It seemed like a good place to start. The next day, we visited the shop and were greeted by the owner, who was very gracious and understanding. As Mom tried on a couple of wigs, the owner's compassion and care became evident. Mom chose a lovely wig that made her look more like herself, and her expression transformed from sadness to smiles. We bought the wig, and Mom's entire demeanor shifted to one of confidence and peace. What a difference it made for both of us.

Years later, after we moved into the lodging facility, I was working in the office when a young nurse came to Victory in the Valley. She was crying because she had just been diagnosed with cancer. Concerned about her finances, as she was single and needed to work to maintain her insurance coverage, she was also grappling with the overwhelming challenges of cancer and treatment. Attractive, with beautiful red hair, she faced mounting bills and decreasing energy levels due to treatment fatigue. As she confronted the prospect of losing her hair, she asked if we had a wig she could use. Since we didn't, I called the shop where Mom had purchased her wig and spoke with the owner about sending us the bill for this young lady's wig. I inquired about opening an account so that if there were others who needed help, we could refer them to her shop and cover the costs. She explained that she couldn't open an account for us as she was retiring and planning to close the shop. I was so disappointed because she was wonderful, and we loved working with her. She mentioned that she would have a closing sale. I told her that if she had anything that didn't sell and wanted to donate it to us, we would provide her with a tax receipt for the items. She asked what we would do with them, and I explained that we would give them to ladies with cancer who needed them.

I became busy with other things, and several months passed. As always, God's timing is perfect.

One day, Cherlyn Fox, the owner of The Wig Shoppe, called me and asked if I could come down to the shop. I agreed and arranged a time to meet. Cherlyn had decided to donate $13,000 worth of wigs, wig stands, hats, turbans, caps, mirrors, furniture, and everything we needed to assist women with cancer when they lose their hair! God had determined we needed a women's boutique, and He made it happen.

Today, our Women's Boutique continues to be busy helping women look and feel better after a cancer diagnosis. All items are provided to patients at no cost.

Later, we were "adopted" by the second graders from Magdalen School, who wanted a tour of Victory in the Valley. The Women's Boutique was one of the stops on the tour, and I delivered my best second-grade discussion about how cancer treatments can cause temporary hair loss. There was a young boy who resembled a character from The Christmas Story movie. He wore glasses, had slicked-down hair, dressed very nicely, and appeared quite intelligent. I asked if any of the kids had questions, and he scanned the room, looking at the shelves lined with heads displaying wigs. He then raised his hand, and I thought, "Oh, this should be a great question coming from him!" He looked again at the faces with wigs on the shelves and asked, "So, who ARE all these people?" I think he felt relieved to learn that they were not real people and that he wasn't going to lose his head!

One day, a middle-aged lady arrived for her appointment at the boutique. She looked very weak and could barely make it up the steps. Clearly, she was struggling emotionally with losing her hair and didn't want to deal with the process of choosing a wig. Our volunteer understood her situation and gently, patiently assisted her in selecting wigs to try on. Suddenly, she stood in front of the mirror with a big smile on her face and exclaimed, "Look at me! Just look at me! Aren't I pretty? I look just like I did before I got cancer! In fact, I look so good that I'm calling my husband, and he's taking me to lunch!" She had no trouble making her way quickly down the steps and out to lunch.

Women's boutique at Victory in the Valley

What a blessing it is to help women feel more normal again. When they find that perfect wig and inquire about the cost, it brings such joy to say that there is no charge.

A few days ago, we received a call from a grandmother whose eighteen-year-old granddaughter had been undergoing treatment for two types of cancer, one after the other. The treatment for the first cancer had been effective. However, in a very short time, she developed a new type of cancer and was currently receiving treatment for it. Although she lost her hair, she looked forward to attending her high school prom and hoped to find something to help her look and feel more normal.

Since they lived some distance from Wichita, we scheduled an appointment that would work for them to visit the Women's Boutique. Imagine my surprise when they arrived; I discovered that her grandmother had been a dear friend of mine for many years, but we had lost touch. What a joyful yet emotional reunion, as we could help this young lady prepare and feel more normal for her big event! Soon, this beautiful, accomplished, sweet young woman emerged from the boutique with a big smile, proudly displaying her new look.

High school cancer patient receives a wig for prom

The three of us sat down and took a few minutes to catch up on life. What an honor and blessing it is to demonstrate God's love by making a practical difference in the lives of those we serve!

More than three hundred women receive wigs, turbans, scarves, hats, and encouragement each year through this free service. I am amazed at how God uses others to meet the practical needs of those enduring such a difficult time.

Yet, we also started to realize that many patients and families still needed support and encouragement that we were not providing. What else could we do?

# 16

In the early 1980s, when both Mom and Linda Richardson were undergoing treatment for cancer, they had to endure various smells, particularly food smells, which made them feel nauseous. Since very few medications could alleviate nausea, many patients struggled to eat at all. When Linda was receiving treatment at MD Anderson in Houston, Texas, the seating arrangement in the chemotherapy infusion room consisted of a wooden school desk and an unpadded chair. During her four to six hours of infusion, her husband, Tom, or her mother also sat at a school desk. If Linda had a scan, she would receive her injection of dye and then wait for an hour or more before having the scan. The only place for her to wait was in the cafeteria, which significantly contributed to her nausea due to the food odors.

After Linda began working at Victory in the Valley, I accompanied her to a patient conference at MD Anderson. It was the 1990s, and the administration of chemotherapy had changed dramatically. A room was established where patients could wait for tests or treatment instead of in the cafeteria. The room was quite small, featuring a little desk, a love seat, and a cooler stocked with juice. It could accommodate only three or four people at most. As we toured the facilities, our guide showed us this waiting room.

Ironically, one of the ladies from the convention placed a small stack of poems on the desk and said, "This is the best poem I have ever read, and each of you needs to take at least one of them!"

I picked one up and realized it was Linda's poem titled "Comforters." I was so excited that I exclaimed loudly, "The lady who wrote this is right here," while pointing to Linda, who was standing behind me in line. My excitement faded when I noticed that the lady had altered the wording of Linda's poem. Linda was not happy when she saw it. She had a brief, private, and very direct conversation with the lady, urging her never to change the poem's wording again or reprint it without permission, as the bottom of the poem card stated, "Reprint with permission only!" (I kept walking.)

On the plane returning home from the conference, we talked about that little room. Linda mentioned that, although it was small, it would have been wonderful to have a similar room while she was receiving treatment instead of sitting in a cafeteria. A small seed was planted, and I made a note to call the building management to inquire about space and costs near the cancer center in Wichita.

The following day, I called to inquire about any vacancies down the hall from the Cancer Center of Kansas office. I asked if there was space available on the fourth floor and was informed that there was none. I continued the conversation regarding any availability in the building, knowing that pursuing this possibility would likely be a waste of time. Again, I asked, "So there is nothing available next to the Cancer Center of Kansas?" She informed me that there was a suite of offices for rent on that floor, but it was reserved for a medical office.

She then asked, "What would you use it for?" I told her about Victory in the Valley. I explained that we needed a spacious room where cancer patients and their families could gather instead of the waiting room, which often feels cold and impersonal during such a frightening time. I also mentioned that we would provide volunteers to offer snacks to the patients and caregivers, creating a quiet space filled with kindness and peace where they could unwind. It was meant to be an "oasis" in the storm of cancer. She responded, "Well, we do have a room available next to the Cancer Center of Kansas, but it is just one large room."

There it was! We had found our hospitality room, and it was even better than the one in Houston! God had shown us what He intended our next service to be.

We settled on a price and signed a lease. Our board members, especially their wives, began decorating and planning what was needed. They donated furniture, coordinated the décor, and transformed the space into a warm, welcoming haven of peace and encouragement. When we informed our volunteers about this next expansion of services, they were extremely excited and volunteered extra days to help. We ordered individually wrapped snacks, coffee, and juice. Best of all, we brought in listening ears and caring hearts from those who had experienced the cancer journey themselves and wanted to give back to others because of what they had received.

Approximately 12,700 cancer patients and caregivers visit the Hospitality Centre each year. Our hospitality staff members, who are cancer survivors, provide hope and encouragement along with snacks.

Since many patients arrive just in time for their appointments at the Cancer Center of Kansas, not all of them visit the Hospitality Centre. Therefore, our

Hospitality Centre – patients relaxing as they wait for appointments

volunteers bring a basket of snacks into the treatment rooms to visit patients during their chemotherapy sessions. This provides a nice break for the patients: receiving encouragement, laughter, and a caring smile along with their snacks. While some patients welcome a visit, others do not; we respect each patient's needs and desires, keeping in mind that they are a captive audience during their treatment, and we follow their lead.

Some patients just want to sleep through their treatment, so we don't disturb them. Other patients enjoy having someone to talk to, whether it's about trying different snacks or sharing the latest jokes. Since taste and appetite can often be challenging, we are pleased to see them enjoying a special treat. Our volunteers average nearly 28,000 visits to the treatment rooms each year in Wichita.

We have additional volunteers who live and serve in other cities throughout Kansas, providing a variety of services. For instance, in Newton, Kansas, they visit cancer patients in local treatment rooms and offer the same support. There, volunteers assist approximately twenty-seven hundred people annually. It is a joy to serve cancer patients and their family members in the smaller communities of our state. The needs of cancer patients are largely the same, particularly in communities that lack access to essential services.

When there is a desire to extend Victory in the Valley's services to smaller communities, we establish chapters. These chapters operate under Victory in the Valley-Wichita and offer our support groups and other services to patients in their respective areas. They adhere to the same requirements and guidelines as the by-laws of Victory in the Valley.

Victory in the Valley will go anywhere to do whatever we can to help those who are struggling, some of whom have no family or support. Serving all cancer patients with any type of cancer continues to be the joy and goal of our organization.

# No one should have to go through cancer alone. How sad that they should try!

Recently, I received a call from a cancer survivor living in a small town in Kansas, about fifty miles from Wichita. She wanted to start a support group in her town and wondered if we could assist her. I explained that we would love to help her establish a chapter of Victory in the Valley. I suggested she reach out to a couple of other survivors or caregivers to see if they were interested in assisting so it wouldn't become burdensome for her and the group meetings wouldn't always rely on her. We will drive down to meet with those interested and help them find encouragement in their own area. What a joy it is to have the opportunity to assist cancer patients and caregivers wherever they live.

Michelle Green volunteers as she visits with patients at Hospitality Centre

# 17

One way we show patients that we care about each of them is by giving them a small stuffed teddy bear- a Victory Bear!

A man came into the treatment room to receive his first chemo treatment. He was alone and looked like a "street person," with his unshaven face and dirty, disheveled clothing. One of our female volunteers approached him gently and offered him a Victory Bear. She wasn't sure what to expect from this tough-looking fellow. As you can imagine, many men are reluctant to accept a stuffed bear. Letting anyone know they just received a teddy bear is not exactly macho! They either say, "No, thank you," or respond with, "I'll give it to my grandchild," which somewhat defeats the purpose.

The volunteer told the man that the bear served as a reminder that Victory in the Valley cared for him and that we were there to support him through his cancer. He grunted, took the bear, and walked away. However, each time he came in for treatment, he came alone- except for his Victory Bear, which he always brought. It served as a reminder that we never know the impact a word or deed offered at just the right moment might have on another person. Our volunteers distribute over 1000 Victory Bears each year. They are always given to patients receiving treatment for the first time as a reminder that they are not alone.

New Patient Bag – Includes Victory Bear, Stitches of Hope quilt and other comfort items

# 18

The Lodge at Victory in the Valley was established to meet the needs of cancer patients seeking a place to stay near their oncology treatments in Wichita. In the early days of Victory in the Valley, only about four or five cities in the entire state offered oncology treatment services. Many cancer patients chose to receive treatment in Wichita, and we were pleased to assist with lodging for those in need.

Thankfully, in recent years, many oncologists have opened satellite offices in smaller communities across Kansas to serve local cancer patients better. While this change has significantly benefited cancer patients, it has led to The Lodge apartments being underused. Although The Lodge's occupancy dropped to nearly zero, our overhead did not decrease.

In 2003, the board decided that we should no longer waste money on maintaining a facility that was no longer necessary. Consequently, the board chose to pursue the sale of The Lodge.

One block south of The Lodge, there was another nonprofit organization, Inter-Faith Ministries, whose mission was to assist the homeless. Their goal was to provide support with lodging and job placement and to teach life skills to mitigate homelessness. When the organization learned we were interested in selling, they initiated discussions about purchasing The Lodge. The price was agreed upon, and the transaction for The Lodge was completed. (Although we no longer have lodging facilities, we continue to provide lodging assistance using selected hotels for cancer patients traveling to Wichita from out of town for treatment.)

Meanwhile, Linda and I lived just a few blocks apart in Wichita and carpooled to work. Our route took us past a stunning three-story house built in 1906. This gorgeous brick home was rumored to have been constructed as a family residence for a man who owned lumber yards. We were told he initially planned to build it for $15,000 but ended up spending double that amount.

It had long been sold by the family, but it had been well cared for. We knew that a group of investors had purchased the property and made it available for rent for weddings, birthday parties, and other events. One of the volunteers from Victory in the Valley celebrated her birthday at this property, and Mom and I were invited to attend. When we stepped inside, we were in awe. The interior was as beautiful as the exterior, featuring leaded glass, stunning wooden beams, and exquisite rooms.

We sat down and looked around. I said, "Mom, wouldn't this be a wonderful place to relocate Victory in the Valley? But I'm sure it would cost more money than we could ever afford." We enjoyed the party, and then each day, as we drove past on our way to work, Linda and I talked about the building and how amazing it would be for Victory in the Valley. After that, every time we drove by the house, I prayed that if God wanted us to have it, it might someday serve as the new location for Victory in the Valley. However, it felt more like wishful thinking, as I hardly believed it could ever become a reality!

In the meantime, the board was exploring options for a smaller facility than The Lodge to better utilize and potentially expand our current services, as we rarely needed to provide lodging for cancer patients. They met with a realtor, Marlin Penner, to investigate other buildings in the community. Board Chairman Britt Fulmer asked me to create a list of features I would like included in a new facility. I wrote down five wishes:

1. A location to expand the Women's Boutique with sufficient storage, allowing us to provide a wide variety of options in wig colors and styles.

2. A place with multiple rooms which would allow us to have more than one meeting simultaneously. We could then add support groups that would meet at various times convenient for more patients.

3. A large meeting room that can accommodate 75 to 100 people, allowing us to begin providing educational sessions on topics related to the practical needs of cancer patients and their caregivers (such as our Lunch & Learns).

4. Because we expanded many of our services, we needed office space to enhance staff productivity by providing them with shared workspace areas.

5. A warm, welcoming, and inviting space where everyone, regardless of their economic status, feels comfortable and valued.

I felt a bit greedy for requesting these items, not truly believing they could become a reality. However, I experienced a sense of peace knowing that no matter how our search ended, the outcome would be wonderful!

Within a week, the realtor contacted us to show us some locations. He mentioned that there were a couple of storefronts that might be available, and I confess I was not very open to that idea, nor were the board members.

Marlin then added, "There is one more place that is not on the market, but when I spoke to them, they were possibly willing to sell. Let's go look at that one if you are interested in seeing it."

We agreed, and as we headed to the next stop, he said, "I think this one might be perfect for you." Imagine my *shock* when he turned into the driveway of the very three-story home that Linda and I passed by every day and had dreamed about! I nearly cried.

We walked up the steps to the beautiful building and went inside. As we looked around (me, through tears), Britt said, "Diana, this is it! Warm, welcoming, and inviting!" Once again, God had done "exceedingly abundantly above all that we ask or think"(Ephesians 3:20 KJV). The board met and voted unanimously to proceed. I was overwhelmed.

Soon, we had a meeting with Inter-Faith Ministries, and they decided to purchase our property. We received their check for the sale of our property. Later, we met with the sellers of the beautiful house. As I wrote the check, along with Mom, Linda, and our board, tears flowed at the amazing and overwhelming goodness of our God!

We named it Victory House.

With the purchase of the beautiful Victorian home, we were able to enhance the landscaping to reflect the house's new purpose.

Victory in the Valley ribbon cutting ceremony at Victory House

Victory House, 3755 E. Douglas, Wichita, KS

# 19

When we moved to Victory House, we established a Cancer Survivor Garden, a Memorial Garden, and a Caregiver Garden. Bricks inscribed with the names of those honored are set into the garden walkway. The gardens provide a beautiful, serene space for reflection and honoring those who have been part of the cancer journey.

We purchased gardening supplies at Tree Top Nursery and Landscape, Inc., a local garden center. The owner inquired about Victory in the Valley and our activities. After learning who we were and the services we provided for cancer patients, he asked how they could assist us, mentioning that they had a dear friend who had just lost her battle with cancer. Soon, they presented us with a project that Tree Top Nursery wanted to undertake in her honor.

After a short time, they were ready to proceed. There was an area on the side of Victory House that was an unnecessary part of the parking lot. Soon, it was removed, and trees and soil were brought in. Flowers and bushes

Victory House: gardens include bricks to honor Survivors, Caregivers & Memorials

were planted, a fence was erected, and the bricks were laid in the new Connie Mills Meditation Garden in honor of their dear friend.

Later, with the help of volunteers, we established a Cancer Survivor Garden to honor those who have battled cancer by inscribing their names on bricks set in the garden.

Cancer survivors requested that we create a Caregiver Garden, allowing them to honor those who supported them during their cancer journey. We agreed and established a third garden to ensure these caregivers received recognition. What a joy it is to see the names of so many who have walked together through the valleys of cancer to victory!

Recently, a pergola was added to the garden and patio area, which features wooden tables, benches, and twinkling lights. This space is designed for support groups to gather, enjoy meals, and encourage one another! Zernco, Inc. organized a fundraiser for us, and we used the proceeds to purchase materials for the pergola. They generously built it at no cost to us, and we proudly placed their name on it in recognition of their donation.

Victory house – gardens and pergola donated by Zernco, Inc.

Lois Thomi memorial brick

# 20

Victory in the Valley supports cancer patients of all types; however, it is primarily women who seek our information and services. Two of our female survivors attended a camp for women with cancer in another state. They returned invigorated and inspired after spending time with other women. Their enthusiasm was so contagious that they convinced us to organize a similar event.

In 2003, we launched a women's weekend retreat, which has been incredibly successful for twenty-three years. As a result, we continue to hold it annually. We have witnessed women who attended our event transform from hopeless to hopeful, discovering the strength to continue their treatment when they were ready to give up. What an honor!

We named our retreat Camp Victory (and no, we do not sleep in tents) and began planning a three-day, two-night experience for up to one hundred female cancer patients and survivors. The long weekend includes cancer-related education, humor, pampering, fun activities, and plenty of laughter!

We also fill the weekend with music. Don and Benita Baker, musicians who have been integral to the organization for years, faithfully attend camp each year to enrich us with wonderful music, a hint of playfulness, and a lot of fun! The Bakers have never missed singing at the Sunday morning celebration, and each year, they fill our hearts with hope and encouragement. They truly make this day a celebration. The Bakers have generously donated proceeds from their musical recordings to Victory in the Valley and continue to bless our community with their musical talents.

The first time I heard them sing was at a wedding, and I thought they had flown in from New York for the occasion. Later, I discovered they lived right here in Wichita and wanted to support Victory in the Valley by singing at our events. Over the years, a sweet friendship has developed, and I am so thankful for their dedication and loyalty to serve whenever needed.

In recent years, we have been blessed by the music of Janet Eldridge. Throughout the weekend, she reminds us through her songs that we are deeply loved by the One who loves us the most. Each morning, her music serves as a prayer of blessing, reminding us that every day is a new gift of life. In the evenings, her songs conclude each day with gratitude for rest and renewal. Her beautiful voice often soothes the stresses of the weekend, bringing God's peace to our hearts.

We conclude the weekend with a survivor ceremony that encourages everyone to embrace life fully every day. It serves as a reminder to release our stresses as we return to the realities of our lives at home. We then finish with a traditional Thanksgiving meal, even though Camp Victory takes place in the spring. This time of gratitude encourages us to appreciate every day of life. What a joy and privilege it is to witness the difference that hope can make.

Women's Weekend committee members (enjoying their time together)

After the "highs" of Women's Weekend, we began reflecting on the importance of hope and how we could communicate it more effectively to our patients throughout the year.

Women's Weekend group picture

# 21

We became acquainted with a quilting group that focused on creating and donating lap quilts to patients. We loved their group's name, Stitches of Hope, and their commitment to reaching out and helping those undergoing treatment. The ladies possess incredible talents and collaborate every week to inspire hope in others by gifting them the beauty and comfort of a lap quilt.

This group soon became very important in contributing to the gift bags we provide for patients. Included in the bag are a neck pillow, information about our services, and a booklet we created called Navigating the Cancer Journey, which offers suggestions and questions to ask their oncologist or nurse. The patient's caregiver also receives their own lap quilt, made by Stitches of Hope, and a booklet we wrote entitled Being an Effective Caregiver, which provides tools for them to support their patient.

The Stitches of Hope quilting group has created over *seven thousand lap quilts* for us to donate to individuals undergoing cancer treatment. This outreach has blessed thousands of patients and caregivers each year, continuing to surround those facing challenging times with comfort, care, and *hope*!

Stitches of Hope: the group of talented quilters who have made over 7,000 quilts for patients

# 22

When word spread about Mom's diagnosis, people began calling and visiting her. Their words often turned the journey into an even greater emotional roller coaster of highs and lows. It felt as though the burden was too heavy to bear.

> I firmly believe that most people who say the wrong thing do not intend to, but instead simply do not quite know what to say.

We felt a kinship with Job's experience in the Bible, where his "comforters" arrived and started providing unwelcome advice. Here are Linda Richardson's insights on the biblical story of Job, his so-called comforters, and how it relates to cancer patients.

## But Poor Job!

Discussion about Job from Cancer Support Group Notes (this section is paraphrased from Job 4-14) by Linda Mae Richardson.

After Job became ill, his friends saw him from a distance and could hardly recognize him. Like cancer, treatment brings many changes: pallor, hair loss, and weight loss are just a few. Often, visitors are shocked at how the cancer patient's appearance has changed, and they do not know what to say. They are uncomfortable, so they often try to be positive and tell the patient how well they look when, in fact, the patient knows the truth. Kindly and yet truthfully, we can assure them that the changes must be so hard but that they are still who they have always been on the inside, and that is who we love and care about.

After a time, Job begins to share his true feelings. He says he has no peace, can't rest, and is depressed, and his days have no meaning for him.

That can often be a normal response to the diagnosis of cancer. As Bob Stephen, a previous Kansas attorney general and cancer survivor, often said, "Why wouldn't you be depressed? Who wants it?"

The patients often look in a mirror and hardly recognize themselves. They sometimes feel their whole identity has been stolen. They feel trapped!

They don't want to go through cancer and treatment, but they want to live. They may feel as though they don't have a choice and are a victim. We consider them a SURVIVOR because they are alive *in spite* of cancer!

Job's friend finally comes to visit him. He basically tells him, "You have always been strong and comforted and built up others, but now, when you are in trouble, why are you so fearful and unhappy? Shouldn't YOU be trusting God?"

Although his friend may have been trying to help Job regain his focus, it is never the time to condemn or point out perceived failures in another. It is a time to **listen**, **encourage**, and **accept** their changing emotions and attitudes as they work through the process. It's hard to be "up" when you are sick and afraid.

Job's friends now try to give him more advice: "Listen to us! If it were me, I would just go to God and quit worrying! Where's your faith anyway?"

Job responds, "I wish my pain and fear could be weighed or measured. If you knew and experienced how I feel, you would understand that it's not as easy as you think!" He tells them that they are worthless physicians, and if only they would be quiet, for you, that would be wisdom!!

During someone's cancer journey, we have the opportunity to listen, support, and care! We can't possibly understand what another person is experiencing, and we don't have the right to minimize their feelings. Obviously, there are differing pain thresholds, so we really can't totally understand. Now, there are those to whom everything is a crisis, but those who struggle with cancer and treatment go through a lot, and their feelings should not be minimized.

The third friend asked Job if he had committed some sin, and if so, he should confess it, and he would get well!

This statement was said to Mom! Her response was, "I have confessed every sin I can think of and some that I haven't even done!" Like the third friend, we are so often quick to judge or to find a reason why someone else is going through illness. We often use Scripture to do it. I fully believe Scripture is our source of hope, strength, and encouragement, and I believe the Lord will give us the right scripture to share at just the right time to encourage, but not because we feel we must find a reason for someone's difficulty.

For example, while Mother was in the hospital, one of her visitors glibly said, "Well, Lois, the Lord gives, and the Lord takes away!" That was not comforting (although true) and was not the time or place to try to use Scripture to give a reason.

One of my family members lost their first child when he was about eighteen months old through an accident. We were all at the hospital waiting on news in the Grief Room. The family's pastor came to the room and began to constantly quote Scripture, quote the words to songs, and more Scripture. (I didn't think he would ever stop talking and walking around.) Soon, it became irritating, and although the scriptures were true, and we all believed them, he never stopped talking. I didn't find it comforting at all, and I'm not sure the parents did either. Then, their family doctor came into the room. He sat down between the parents and put his arms around each of them. He didn't speak for a time but just held them as they cried, and he shed tears with them. *That is a comforter!* Many times, it is our actions, not just our words, that can bring comfort.

Linda's (paraphrase) teaching continues:

One of Job's friends said, "If your faith is strong and you are pure and upright, God will restore you. (This was also said to my mother.) Job's response was,

'No matter what I do or say, I can never be perfect or blameless in God's sight' (paraphrase of Job 9:20).

Aren't we thankful that God's love for us doesn't depend on our goodness but on His great love for us?

Job's friends essentially said, "Why are you angry with God, and why would you question Him?"

Job replied, "I've heard this before! All of you are terrible at comforting me! Your long-winded speeches go on forever- won't they ever end? What is wrong with you, and why do you keep on arguing? You are all worthless physicians!! If you were silent, for you, that would be wisdom!" Job concluded, "My friends scorn me, but my eyes pour my tears to God!"

(Paraphrases: Job16:1-3; 13:5; 16:20)

Many times, amid our troubles in this life, it ultimately comes down to the fact that people often let us down, but God is our refuge, who will never fail. He keeps all our tears in a bottle, regardless of the cause of our tears. He loves us, and we are *that* precious to Him.

As we visit those experiencing crises, a good question to consider is:

What is the best way to express love, compassion, and sympathy for someone who is hurting?

Charles Swindoll, a well-known author and pastor, recommends four practices that are helpful for those who are struggling (*Growing Strong in the Seasons of Life* by Charles R. Swindoll, c1983):

**"BE REAL!** As you reach out, be honest and admit your honest feelings to them."

**"BE QUIET!** Your presence, not your words, will be what is most appreciated."

"(Don't try to answer the "why's" or offer explanations and reasons. We don't know!)"

**"BE SUPPORTIVE!** Those who comfort must have a tender heart of understanding."

**"BE AVAILABLE!** (If you offer help to the patient or family, be sure to follow through.)"

---

The following is an example from one of our Cancer Support Group Meetings:

Attending this one meeting, in particular, was a ninety-year-old man and a young nurse just starting her career, both of whom had cancer. We watched as the age barrier was crossed in a comforting, tender way. The older gentleman approached the young nurse, who was crying, and said to her, "I can't begin to understand what you must be feeling, but I want you to know that I care about everything you feel!" He was a comforter- no reasons, no quotes, no answers to the 'whys,' just caring, listening, and kindness.

# Knowledge is knowing WHAT to say. Wisdom is knowing whether or not to say it!

While undergoing cancer treatment, the patient and their family can experience significant stress, making them particularly sensitive to the words of others. Often, friends and family have good intentions, but they are usually unaware of the challenges the patient is facing.

One of the most difficult challenges for protective family members is avoiding feelings of anger towards those who say hurtful or insensitive things, especially when they are unaware of how it may sound to those deeply involved in the battle against cancer. The patient and family may carry emotions of anger and hurt from what was said, while the well-intentioned person who made the remark has no idea how it sounded or how it was received. Often, it's simply that they don't know what to say.

## Remember: Life becomes easier when you learn to accept the apology you never got!

This poem, titled "Comforters," written by Linda Mae Richardson, serves as one of the best reminders of the impact of our words:

**COMFORTERS**

When I was Diagnosed with Cancer:

My first friend came and expressed his shock by saying, "I can't believe that you have cancer. I always thought you were so active and healthy."

He left, and I felt alienated and somehow very "different."

My second friend came and brought me information about different treatments being used for cancer. He said, "Whatever you do, don't take chemotherapy. It's a poison!"

He left, and I felt scared and confused.

My third friend came and tried to answer my "whys?" with the statement, "Perhaps God is disciplining you for some sin in your life."

He left, and I felt guilty.

My fourth friend came and told me, "If your faith is just great enough, God will heal you."

He left and I felt my faith must be inadequate.

My fifth friend came and told me to remember that "All things work together for good."
He left, and I felt angry.
My sixth friend never came at all.
I felt sad and alone.
My seventh friend came and held my hand and said, "I care, I'm here, I want to help you through this."
He left, and I felt loved!

As the poem states, to be a true comforter, your main task is to care and be present. Caring takes many forms, but it is primarily best expressed in the words, "How can I help?" When an answer is given, be ready to act! There is nothing more hurtful than when a patient or family member opens up and allows someone to assist with a task, only for that task to be forgotten. Nothing can make someone feel more alone than being overlooked or feeling insignificant. For the patient, when you allow someone to help you, you gift them the opportunity to bless you.

The fact remains that no matter how many "comforters" accompany someone along the way, the journey must be taken by the cancer patient alone. It is he or she who must undergo each treatment, experience the side effects, and endure the roller coaster of physical ups and downs. The emotional side effects are felt by everyone in the inner "circle of caring," often resulting in feelings of frustration and helplessness for everyone involved in the journey.

Mom's advice on how to help people with cancer:

- Don't treat them with pity.
- Don't treat them like they are going to die.
- Don't say "call if you need something;" make the offer specific.
- Don't talk, listen!
- Guard your ears and mouth.
- Don't try to explain why things happen.
- Don't make them feel guilty, like they have done something wrong.
- Be real, say the word "cancer."
- Ask them how they are doing, but don't make them talk.

"Our thoughts can drain our energy and cripple our usefulness. Thoughts can be turned around and be the source of strength when we let God work through these truths and change our thinking."

When Mom first began speaking to groups about her cancer journey, she used the motto:

## "When you have cancer, prepare to die, then plan to live."

# 23

As a nurse, oncology held a special place in my heart. Although it was often heart-wrenching, I considered it an honor to be part of a family's cancer journey. However, I also learned that the experience is very different when it involves your own family. I tried to remain objective, but I felt what many caregivers feel. I realized that while many cancer patients initially feel hopeless, their caregivers often feel helpless!

Although I knew better, I began to "smother" Mom by hovering over her, which undoubtedly added to her stress. One day, she reminded me that she was still the mother and that I didn't need to be there all the time; I needed to give her a break. She strongly suggested that I go do something fun. As much as I felt guilty for leaving her, I called my friend Charlene Jantz, and we went to dinner. We laughed and talked about life, and when it was time to leave, I realized how much better I felt. The fun that followed was worth it all, as I shared some of the funny things we talked about with Mom, which made her world seem bigger and much more interesting.

I was reminded of how much the diagnosis and treatment of cancer is a family journey. Everyone reacts or responds based on who they are and their comfort levels, which can complicate matters even further. Some patients or family members need to discuss the situation, whereas others prefer not to talk or share their feelings at all. Some wish to be completely involved in each appointment or conversation, while others feel they can't even show up. Some need to feel in control, and while some patients appreciate that, others feel bossed around and resent not being allowed to have an opinion.

When a patient or family member is used to being in control, losing that control during cancer can be very challenging, leading them to exert excessive control in other areas. Family dynamics often undergo changes, resulting in stressful times, as the patient may seem like a different person. It is crucial for family and friends to allow the patient to take the lead and to listen rather than provide unsolicited advice or opinions. I encourage them to share and, whenever possible, support the patient's decisions regarding their situation. While it can be helpful to offer suggestions for the patient's consideration, it is important not to feel upset if the patient disagrees. Difficult conversations can become much easier for the entire family if everyone remains flexible, kind, supportive, and loving to the one who matters most. Ultimately, regardless of family consensus, it is the patient who must be heard.

Since Mom had a wonderful sense of humor, when people asked what they could do for her, I suggested they send a funny card or something humorous that she would appreciate to let her know they cared. The weight of fear often lightens with laughter. While this approach may not work for everyone, it's important to encourage whatever gifts the patient enjoys during these particularly challenging times. More importantly, be present for what matters to them and share your own gifts and talents as well.

Caregivers must also find ways to attend to their physical and emotional needs. You can become the support and motivation you need by first taking care of yourself. Allow someone else to take your place for a while and do something enjoyable, share lunch with a friend, or run errands. If necessary for the patient's care and safety, arrange for someone to stay with them. It's beneficial to let the patient choose someone they feel comfortable with and enjoy. Both of you will benefit from feeling refreshed and taking a break!

I remember when Mom was in the hospital early in her treatment. We had always enjoyed so much fun together and shared a lot of laughter. But that night was different. I came to visit her and spend the evening there. It had been a horrible day for her, so we were both quiet.

I was worried, and she was afraid, yet we both talked around it. I went to the window and noticed a family getting into their car after visiting hours. They were laughing contagiously with one another and having fun. I felt so angry to see them happy since our world had been turned upside down; I thought there was nothing to laugh about. I also remembered how ridiculous my response was, but it was still how I felt. I realized how long it had been since we had laughed together.

Later, something goofy happened in Mom's room that struck both Mom and me as funny, and we started to laugh hysterically. I remember how good it felt to enjoy a normal, hearty laugh during such an abnormal, heavy time.

Family members often become protective of the patient, who, in turn, becomes protective of their family. The patient may hesitate to express true feelings or needs for fear of being a burden. Each individual navigates feelings of hurt, anger, and fear to avoid making things seem worse. Maintaining a sense of normalcy after a cancer diagnosis is challenging because the old "normal" is lost. Former routines become irrelevant, leading to a frightening and confusing time. Caregivers and patients must work together to adapt to a new schedule, which may involve changing job situations or redefining roles within the family.

After a cancer diagnosis, many people feel compelled to evaluate or make changes in their lives and attitudes. It's even more beneficial to periodically evaluate ourselves without facing a crisis. Often, we overlook the blessings that God intends for us because we become so caught up in life and pursue our own agendas. This distraction can cause us to lose our perspective and our "Attitude of Gratitude." A poem by Linda Mae Richardson serves as a valuable reminder.

## WISDOM

At the end of my days, I hope to look back
Not to number my days or simply keep track.
Though we hope for a life which is healthy and strong
It is sad if we see just a life that was long.

For our number of days, short or long was a gift!
Did I use them with wisdom to help and uplift?
A life filled with meaning adds width to its days
Years filled with love lived by faith and with praise.

Lord, teach me to measure – Your thoughts as my guide,
Then I'll look back on life and thank God mine was wide!

# 24

After being a part of my mom's experience with cancer and working with Victory in the Valley for the past 41 years, I have learned a great deal from those enduring some of the most challenging days of their lives. I have come to understand that we should always remain open to learning and should not wait for a crisis in our lives to do so.

I have learned that we are not cookie-cutter people, and there are no exact right or wrong ways of doing things. I have witnessed fear, helplessness, and anger; I have encountered some caring individuals who do everything wrong and others who do everything right. There isn't a manual for "doing cancer," but in each situation, there are life lessons to be learned. I have included the following lessons as "food for thought" from those who are fighting to live. Often, we become consumed by whatever is happening at the moment, and it begins to shape every aspect of our days and lives. We need to keep our priorities in focus and not allow cancer or anything else to control our lives. I hope that some of the things I have included remind us of how to truly live and encourage us not to lose sight of living fully.

It's been said that "you may have cancer, but don't let cancer have you!" This also applies to other obstacles we allow to interfere with our lives. We can learn from these unexpected challenges, and although they may be difficult and even frightening, perhaps those lessons can serve as an anchor to help us build a new foundation for living each day to the fullest.

## Attitude

Our attitudes influence our behavior and actions. When we care for ourselves and others, we uncover hidden treasures: our relationships are strengthened, our self-worth is enhanced, and we gain inner strength from the assurance that God has promised never to leave or abandon us (Hebrews 13:5 NIV). This empowers us to cope better with the unknown and unwanted situations we may encounter. Ultimately, it all comes down to an attitude adjustment.

Charles Swindoll wrote the following about Attitude:

*The longer I live, the more I realize the impact of attitude on life. Attitude, to me, is more important than facts. It is more important than the past, than education, than money, than circumstances, than failures, than successes, than what other people think or say or do. It is more important than appearance, giftedness, or skill. It will make or break a company...a church...a home. The remarkable thing is we have a choice every day regarding the attitude we will embrace for that day. We cannot change our past...we cannot change the fact that people will act in a certain way. We cannot change the inevitable. The only thing we can do is play on the one string we have, and that is our attitude...I am convinced that life is 10% what happens to us and ninety percent how we react to it. And so, it is with you...we are in charge of our Attitudes.*

(Swindoll; *Great Attitudes! 10 Choices for Success in Life* c2006)

Remember: "Holding on to anger is like drinking poison and expecting the other person to die."

—Unknown

We can face, accept, and accomplish many things by framing them in the short term. We can endure a lot that we don't like for just one day. By doing this, we may discover that in the long term, we have even changed our attitudes and actions for the better.

An exercise that might be helpful is to frame the issues of life in terms of how we will live today. Here are some suggestions to say out loud; feel free to create your own:

JUST FOR TODAY, "I will try to live through this day only and not tackle my whole life problems at once."

JUST FOR TODAY, "I will adjust myself to what is, and not just to my desires."

JUST FOR TODAY, "I will not become irritable because of another person who irritates me."

JUST FOR TODAY, "I will do at least two things I don't want to do. (Such as exercise!)"

JUST FOR TODAY, "I will take a 'time out' to get the right perspective before I act."

⚊⚊⚊

A formula for change is as easy as A, B, C! It starts with us, not with our expectations of others.

(A) Attitude Adjustment + (B) Behavioral Changes = (C) Caring for Ourselves and Others. Mom always maintained a positive attitude and rarely felt sorry for herself. She accepted whatever came her way and sought to find the silver lining, even when circumstances were tough. Although she did not look forward to receiving treatment, she underwent it because she understood it was her best chance of survival. She did not dwell in her sadness and avoided wasting time worrying. Instead, she looked for opportunities to help and encourage others on their cancer journey. When we shift our focus away from our own experiences and observe those around us, we can discover that there are always others facing challenges that seem much more difficult than what we are facing.

## Worry

Worry is a natural response to life's crises. Many of us stress over things that may seem insignificant, but to us, they feel monumental. The more we dwell on these worries, the larger they grow. Soon, we can't sleep; we feel nauseated, stressed, and irritable, and life appears completely out of control. The physical symptoms can intensify, making it difficult to handle even the smallest challenges. Worry can become overwhelming and hard to overcome, especially when facing a diagnosis of cancer or other life-threatening illnesses. The hardest part is letting go of all the things that "might" happen.

Someone wisely said that if we have one foot in tomorrow and one foot in yesterday, we will have nothing with which to walk through today. Often, yesterday is rooted in guilt. We spend our time and energy filled with regrets until it monopolizes our days.

Tomorrow is often rooted in fear. It's the "what-ifs" that keep our focus on what might happen. As a result, we miss out on today, allowing both guilt and fear to fill us with worry. The secret is to be thankful and concentrate on today! Each day holds blessings if we take the time to look for them. Counting our blessings enriches each day and helps us overcome worry and fear.

I love the following poem written by Linda Mae Richardson:

**WORRY'S HOLD**
Worry comes like a thief in the night...
Seeking to harm those most vulnerable
Breaking through doors I thought secure...
Enter my home without warning.
Footprints mark a trail of destruction...
In a home stripped of peace and calm
Where worry now claims possession...
Courage is a captive of fear
But worry shall not the victor be...

For I have found new strength within
To break the chains of worry's hold
And claim the blessings of this day!

⁂

Looking back, even long before Mom's cancer diagnosis, we could see how faithful God had always been, particularly during difficult times.

I remember when we first moved to Texas so Dad could become the director of a Rescue Mission there. Shortly after settling in, we discovered it was an unpaid position. We used all the money from Dad's coin collection and had nothing left for food. Dad quoted a scripture that said, "I was young, and now I am old, yet I have never seen the righteous forsaken or their children begging bread." (Psalm 37:25 NIV). I was in the sixth grade and worried that we would soon starve to death! (We weren't even close to that, but I still worried!)

We prayed and asked God, who is the same God in the Bible who took the loaves and fishes to feed five thousand people, to provide for us as well. After we finished the prayer, I asked Dad, "What do we do now?" He replied, "We wait and see how God answers." I wondered how long we would have to wait; I was getting hungry!

Suddenly, there was a knock at the door, and a lady we had met only once stood there, holding two large bags. She was from a local church we had recently visited. She said, "I hope I won't offend you, but I felt compelled to bring you some groceries!" "Offend us?" I thought, "I want you to be our new best friend!"

At our usual mealtime that evening, we enjoyed minute steaks and potatoes with gravy, and there was even a jar of green olives! I loved green olives, but we never bought them because of the extra cost. That night, I felt a special gratitude because the God who loves us all had impressed upon that lady to buy a jar of green olives just for me!

## Hope

The diagnosis of cancer often comes unexpectedly. Immediately upon hearing the word "cancer," fear arises from the unknown. Our thoughts scatter in a million directions, and everything feels out of control. We often turn to "Dr. Google" for reassurance but frequently discover even more reasons for alarm. We start to believe that the life we have known is suddenly coming to an end. There is no hope! We feel overwhelmed. Even Scripture tells us in Proverbs, "Hope deferred makes the heart sick, but a longing fulfilled is a tree of life" (Proverbs 13:12, NIV). We are desperately searching for someone to give us hope.

Hope is a powerful and necessary ingredient for life. The loss of hope is serious because a hopeless person often becomes helpless. Our body, mind, and spirit are all affected when we are ill. Our body, mind, and spirit are also influenced by hope or the absence of it. The healing process from sickness or cancer is shaped by medications and treatment as well as by our emotions and thoughts.

The following paragraph illustrates a perfect example of the influence our thought processes can exert directly on our physical body.

Envision a large, plump yellow lemon. The lemon is round and yellow, feeling firm yet juicy to the touch. As you peel back the outer skin, it reveals a whitish layer that tastes intensely bitter. Peeling through that layer uncovers a juicy center. The lemon emits a pleasant citrus fragrance, and as it sprays a fine mist onto your tongue, you savor a tangy juice that is so sour it makes your lips pucker.

Did you notice a physical sensation in your mouth as you imagined this item? This is a small example of how the mind can influence our body and emphasizes the significance of our thoughts!

Dr. Shaker Dakhil, an oncologist in Wichita, shared the following insights:

"While dealing with terminal cancer patients for twenty years, I frequently have been faced with the following dilemma: how to be truthful to the patients and tell it like it is and, at the same time, avoid destroying their hopes and plunging them into despair."

In an article about the difference between hope and expectation, Dr. Dakhil uses the analogy of a lottery ticket.

*If you buy a lottery ticket, you certainly do not expect to win, but you hope to hit the jackpot and beat all odds. You continue to hope until the drawing is over. Similarly, as long as there is life, there is hope- even though the expectations for recovery might be poor. See, there is a difference between the concept of expectations and the concept of hope. When I talk to patients now, I explain to them clearly what to "expect" from our scientific treatments, what to "expect" during the course of their illness, and the "expected" outcome of their disease. But "hope" is much more than dry, scientific facts. "Hope" relates primarily to one's religious beliefs and roots. Expectations and hope-what a difference a word can make.*

From the booklet *Hanging on to Hope Through a Serious Illness* (Author unknown; written by a cancer survivor).

Here are thoughts from an anonymous cancer survivor:

· "Be Kind to Yourself! You have value simply because you are YOU, not because of what you do!

· Although a fighting spirit makes a difference, don't make things impossible by believing your attitude is everything. You can't control everything.

· Be thankful for each day and greet it joyously. Live life to the fullest!

· Turn to your faith! I guess, often, we don't think we need God until we run into trouble. I've learned how vulnerable we are, how our lives are in God's hands.

· Your friends will stand by you, but God will surround you! "...God has said, 'Never will I leave you; never will I forsake you.' So we say with confidence, 'The Lord is my helper; I will not be afraid. What can mere mortals do to me?' "(Hebrews 13:5-6 NIV).

· Search for meaning from your adversity. We can find meaning and hope even in our darkest days. I didn't ask for this painful experience. But I can choose my response to it. TAKE HEART–by facing death, I learned how to live."

*"It has been said that we may not all get well from cancer, but we can all be healed. Healing doesn't mean that the damage never existed. It means that the damage no longer controls our lives!"* — Anonymous

Linda Mae Richardson shared her thoughts on the importance of healing in mind, body and spirit:

*Emotional healing is as important as physical healing. There are those who are healed physically but remain wounded in mind and spirit. There are also those who may never experience physical healing but who live the healthiest of lives in both their thinking and their joyful spirit. They are LIVING! Being healed physically but remaining wounded in mind and spirit does not bring peace, joy, or happiness.*

## LOVE – FAITH – HOPE
by Linda Mae Richardson

Sometimes I wake up in the night
So paralyzed by fear.
Surprised, I find my shaking hand
Has brushed away a tear.

Then suddenly, I'm wide awake.
Awareness seeping in –
"Oh no, dear God, I cannot face
This cancer once again!"
Then, all the thoughts I dread the most
Keep going through my mind.
I toss and turn for hours
But no comfort can I find.

Then, when I finally cease to fight
This battle all alone –
And offer up a prayer for help
Your love for me is shown.
I come to know a special peace
The world can never give.
God tells me not to fear my death
Which frees me now to live.
And thank you, Lord, for showing me
Together, we can cope.
A new day filled with all Your love –
With faith and trust and hope!

# 25

Do you remember when you were a child and had the fortune to visit an amusement park? Can you recall the lights, the music, and the delightful scents of cotton candy, popcorn, and hot dogs blending together? What an exhilarating time it was! If you were like me, you could never get to the rides fast enough or make them last long enough.

The highlight of the day would be a grand finale ride of such proportions that it almost made one feel sick to think about it: the roller coaster! I would watch it climb to heights unknown until it nearly disappeared into the clouds. Then it would begin to turn downward toward the ground, slowly at first, as if, for a second, it were hanging in thin air. Suddenly, it seemed as though the whole universe was filled with screams as the string of cars seemingly fell toward the earth, only to recover just in the nick of time! What a frightening yet exhilarating experience! You would feel fear like you had never known before, and the knot in your stomach would nearly make you sick. Your future seemed uncertain as you entered unknown territory with that first climb. After you survived the drop, you would recover, feeling relieved and fully alive, only to begin the next ascent and repeat the process.

Isn't this like the cancer experience? At the time of diagnosis, a knot the size of a mountain forms in your stomach, making you feel completely sick! What lies ahead looms large and feels insurmountable. The obstacle before you seems too big, too hard, and too impossible to climb, yet all you can do is face it! You are confronted with the unfamiliar and unknown; you are strapped in against your will, unable to get off this ride. Time stands still while everything around you is in motion, and you are carried along with it. All you can do at this point is HANG ON!

Experiencing cancer, much like a roller coaster ride, is a journey filled with highs and lows, good times and bad, laughter and sadness, much of which is beyond our control.

The secret is not to let the "highs" become overly important or to allow the "lows" to take us to the depths of discouragement. Somewhere in the middle, enjoying each moment and every day, rejoicing in the good and not despairing over the not-so-good, lies the richness of life. Those who have faced their mountain are the most fully alive!

# 26

Whatever mountain you have faced or are currently facing in your life- the difficulties or hardships you never thought you could overcome- don't let them go to waste. Use your story as encouragement and a blessing to someone else confronting their own challenges. By sharing what you've learned, you become a source of encouragement in the lives of others. My hope in sharing the story of Mom and Victory in the Valley is to inspire you.

I'm reminded of an experience from when I was a very little girl. I was at the grocery store with Mom and wanted to buy some candy. She gave me a dime, and I began to cry. I wanted a nickel because I thought it was larger so I could buy more candy! My perception was that I needed something bigger to make me happy, yet the smaller dime was much more valuable. What an example of God, who loves us so much that He often gives us more than we could ever ask for.

One of Linda Mae Richardson's first poems:

**VICTORY**

The battle has begun, Lord

I have not asked for it—nor wanted it.

My shield is tarnished,

My sword is dull.

Lord, clothe me with Your amour.

How perfectly it fits and protects me.

With Your strength, I will stand,

With Your courage, I will fight.

The battle may be won or lost

But Victory is ours!

This heartfelt message was created by a vibrant and intelligent 21-year-old who was a cherished member of our support group and ultimately faced her battle with cancer. Although she is no longer with us, her words continue to inspire:

*Live in the present, not the past. The past is over and cannot be relived...take time to smell the flowers, breathe the fresh air, and look at the beauty that surrounds you. It is all God's artwork. Do not be possessive. Be happy with what you have. Do not be angry for what you do not have. There are others who can only dream of having half of what you have. Having Jesus in your heart is the most valuable possession that you can have. Be happy for all* of the things that you can do, instead of being angry for what you cannot do...material things can always be taken away from you tomorrow, and so can your health. Treat others as if it is the last time you will see them, they could be dead tomorrow. Follow God, and you cannot go wrong.

While I must admit I have not always followed these rules myself, I wish that I had. I know God is in my heart, and I feel a sense of peace coming over me. I have joy and happiness in my heart that I cannot explain. Remember that I love you all, but if it is my turn to go, then I must go.

I get to see Jesus and know what He looks like.

This is something I know that you do not, but I will be waiting.

We can all be together again in Heaven!!

Love, Steph
(1971-1992)

# 27

Mom, who was "supposed" to live only a few months, actually lived thirty-one years after her cancer diagnosis. She stayed actively involved in all the moves and activities of Victory in the Valley, even after I took over as Executive Director. She enjoyed volunteering in our Hospitality Room and sharing her story with cancer patients whenever possible. As far as we know, she lived longer than any woman the doctors were aware of who had been diagnosed with Inflammatory Breast Cancer. Her life was not easy, but she placed her trust in the Lord and looked to Him during the hard times, and there were plenty of those!

Ironically, Dad met Jesus in heaven first. At eighty-three, he developed a growth about the size of a half dollar on his head. It was sarcoma cancer, which continued to spread internally until it affected his esophagus and lungs. He could no longer eat and went home to be with the Lord in August 2003.

Mom developed early dementia shortly after Dad died, so we sold their house, and she moved in with me. We traveled to many places Mom had always wanted to see, and we laughed and experienced many new things that she truly enjoyed. She also kept up with everything happening at Victory in the Valley and loved visiting and sharing her story with newly diagnosed patients. Although she missed Dad, she was able to enjoy experiences she had never had before; she wasn't finished living; she was busier than ever. Eventually, Mom's dementia worsened, and I had to place her in a care facility for her safety. She became great friends with the other ladies there. They often shared the same stories multiple times; the endings were always new for all of them!

I was with Mom when she passed away in 2013 at the age of eighty-six.

We shared lunch on Mother's Day and had wonderful conversations. The next day, she became unresponsive; her organs were failing. There was so much I wanted to say, and I longed to hear her laugh one more time, but that was not to be. I was holding her hand when her eyes flew open. She squeezed my hand, turned her head, looked up into the upper corner of the hospital room, took a breath, and went to her heavenly home to be with her Lord and Savior and with Dad. I miss her every day, but I don't wish her back, as she is with the One who gave His life for her, not just for her but for ALL who believe and receive Him. Because of His death on the cross, I know I will see her and be with her and Dad forever. It's because of His sacrifice and love for all of us, and when we have received Jesus as our Savior, we will spend eternity with the One who loves us most!

**Two of Mom's favorite scriptures:**

Psalm 41:1 KJV:

> *Blessed is he that considereth the poor:*
> *the LORD will deliver him in time of trouble.*

(Mom considered working at the Rescue Mission as a qualification for this verse!)

Psalm 48:14 KJV:

> *For this God is our God for ever and ever:*
> *He will be our guide even unto death.*

**Two of Mom's favorite quotes:**

> "God does not comfort us to make us
> comfortable, but to make us comforters."
> —Dr. Jowett

> "I know where I'm going, but I'm not homesick."
> —Lois Thomi

After nearly thirty years at various Rescue Missions and then founding Victory in the Valley, Mom shared these words that she lived by:

"Life's storms come. Often, we do not know why certain things happen. Although I am now free of cancer in my life, I still experience the hills and the valleys in good times and difficult times. The mountains seem like such a wonderful, refreshing, problem-free place to be. Though we all love and enjoy the mountaintop experiences, it is 'in the valley' where we really grow. The valley is sometimes dark, sometimes lonely, sometimes seemingly hopeless, but the valley is also the place where we learn to trust God. We learn to pray, and we learn to snatch 'victory' from desperate situations. We learn that God is truly God of the valleys and of the hills. When we know Him, He will walk the journey with us, whether the journey is through the hills or the valleys. We *never* walk alone."

# We are sweetly reminded that God has hidden treasures in the valleys and grace in the shadows.

After forty-one years at Victory in the Valley, I stepped down as Executive Director at the end of 2024 and retired. My cousin, Eunice May, who has worked in various capacities at Victory in the Valley for over twenty-five years, has accepted the role of executive director. Her mother, my mom's sister, battled cancer, and Eunice's extensive experience has fully prepared her for this responsibility. It is a privilege and a blessing to know that the baton is being passed on to continue the legacy of Lois and Diana Thomi.

Eunice May (left), current Executive Director of Victory in the Valley

From humble beginnings in our small living room with a few cancer patients and caregivers, as well as a plate of cookies, Victory in the Valley has been blessed to serve thousands of cancer patients throughout Kansas and many other states. It is all because of one woman's heart of compassion, her sense of humor in the midst of hardships, and her faithful dedication to the Lord that Victory in the Valley continues today.

Remember: Today, we are all 100% alive, so don't waste it!

# Wishing you blessings and so many 100% days!

# More on Victory in the Valley

Victory in the Valley's Mission Statement is:

> "To accompany cancer patients and their
> families on their journey by offering hope
> through emotional and spiritual support
> while providing practical services to
> improve the quality of their lives."

Eighty-seven cents of every donated dollar is used to directly serve cancer patients through our free services, which include Transportation, Grocery Assistance, Prescription Assistance, Lodging Assistance & Fuel Vouchers, Women's Boutique, Loaner Medical Equipment and Supplies, New Patient Gift Bags, Victory Bears, Hospitality Centre, Cancer Support Groups, Phone/E-mail/Prayer Support and Canine Friends (the Therapy Dog Program).

The continuation of Victory in the Valley and all our services is a living tribute to Lois Joy Thomi, who understood that the joy and hope we give away to others not only bless them but also return to bless the giver.

Victory in the Valley is a private non-profit organization in Wichita, Kansas, founded in 1984 to support cancer patients and their families both spiritually and emotionally, as well as to meet practical needs. We are entirely funded through donations, memorials, and non-federally funded grants, which allows us to provide all patient services free of charge. We offer support programs and services to cancer patients and caregivers in Wichita and throughout Kansas. The heart and success of Victory in the Valley comes from providing encouragement and hope.We are honored and blessed to serve those who need our services. The Lord, in all that He does, knew there was a need, and in our humility, we stand beside those who cannot stand for themselves. We love you and will continue to serve for as long as He will have us.

I want to express my heartfelt gratitude to the thousands of volunteers who have supported us throughout the years, along with our wonderful small staff. Your contributions mean the world to us, and please know that we could never have achieved this without your passion for the Lord and your dedication to serving others.

**Cookies and Cancer— What a Party!**

For more information or to send much
appreciated donations, contact:

**Victory in the Valley. Inc**.

3755 East Douglas Ave., Wichita, KS 67218

(316) 682-7400, <u>www.victoryinthevalley.org</u>

Janet M. Eldridge is an accomplished professional with a heart for service and a talent for organization. She earned her associate's degree from Friends University and has spent the past 19 years as an Executive Assistant at Lewis & Associates, where her expertise and dedication play a vital role in the company's success. In addition to her professional career, Janet serves on the Board of Directors for Victory in the Valley, Inc.

Beyond her work and community involvement, Janet cherishes time with her family. She and her husband, Mark, have been happily married for 40 years and are the proud parents of three grown children. Their greatest joy is being grandparents to three wonderful little ones who live in Wichita and fill their lives with love and laughter. Janet also considers it a privilege to share her musical gifts at church and in the community, using music as a way to uplift and inspire others.

Diana K. Thomi is a native Kansan. She was born in McPherson, and after graduating high school, she relocated to Wichita to attend Wesley School of Nursing, fulfilling her lifelong dream of becoming a nurse. After completing the program and receiving her RN, B.S., Diana held several leadership positions at Wesley Medical Center, including oncology. Later, Diana  was recruited to join the faculty of the School of Nursing, where she loved teaching others.

Following her mother's diagnosis of cancer, Diana began assisting her by reaching out to other cancer patients and their families with support and hope. These acts of kindness and caring led to the founding of Victory in the Valley, Inc. Today, this nonprofit comprehensive cancer support organization provides free support services to over 100,000 cancer patients and families across Kansas each year.

Diana has received numerous awards throughout her professional career. In 1996, she was one of ten nurses selected from across Kansas to receive the prestigious Nursing the Heart of Healthcare Award from the University of Kansas.

Diana's experiences as a nurse and caregiver for her parents have given her a unique ability to understand and comfort others. Her gifts of compassion, empathy, and fun-loving humor offer encouragement to those seeking answers during their cancer journey. Diana has counseled and guided thousands of patients and caregivers and remains a vital part of speaking to individuals and groups to encourage and share HOPE!

www.ingramcontent.com/pod-product-compliance
Lightning Source LLC
Chambersburg PA
CBHW061742120626
46550CB00005B/1856